The Early Childhood Teacher's

# EVERY-DAY-
# ALL-YEAR-LONG

## Book Of Units, Activities, and Patterns

by
Imogene Forte

Incentive Publications, Inc.
Nashville, TN

*Illustrations and cover by Susan Eaddy*
*Edited by Sally Sharpe*

ISBN 0-86530-041-0

# Table of Contents

## SCIENCE

## MATH

# ABOUT THIS BOOK

Teachers of young children are very special people. THE EARLY CHILDHOOD TEACHER'S EVERY-DAY-ALL-YEAR-LONG BOOK of Units, Activities and Patterns is designed to help make the early childhood teacher's time in the classroom easier and more exciting. This book is a collection of . . .

- skills-based and enrichment teaching units
- group and individual projects
- learning centers
- free-choice interest centers
- holiday, special day, rainy day, and ordinary day activities
- ready-to-use work sheets
- take-home booklets
- stories, songs, poems and puppets
- annotated lists of books to read
- games to play
- hundreds of creative things to make and do, plus
- the teacher's quick-and-easy-year-long planning guide

The ready-to-use planning guide has been developed to simplify planning and preparation for the busy teacher — from the first day of school to the last. Nine monthly calendars are accompanied by specific suggestions for selecting and scheduling learning centers, short and long-range projects, and skills-based and enrichment activities (complete with page number references and additional ideas). Reproducible seasonal patterns, awards, and section pages (designed to be used as booklet covers) complete this bonus section, making it an invaluable tool for every day, all year long!

# SOCIAL AWARENESS

# SOCIAL AWARENESS

INTERNATIONAL DAY
- Wear the dress of your country
- Share a custom - such as: food, dance, art, stories or music.

AFRICA  PERU  THAILAND

Ms. Cravens Kindergarten

The world in which today's child will grow up is a large and complex one indeed. It is a world of television, radio, video, computers, books, magazines, and other printed materials. In this media-saturated environment, the child is exposed at an early age to a phenomenal accumulation of ideas and impressions. It becomes increasingly important to plan programs to help the child develop the skills and concepts necessary for sorting out and making meaningful use of this vast avalanche of scattered information.

The child should be helped to become aware of the many people, places, and things, with all of their similarities and differences, which are a part of this world. Helping a child make sense of his or her place in a sometimes overwhelming environment encourages a healthy respect for others as well as a strong self-concept. This in turn provides the basis for the development of knowledge, responsibility, cooperation, and the blossoming of the child's creative potential.

# THINGS TO DO TO HELP CHILDREN DEVELOP SOCIAL AWARENESS SKILLS AND CONCEPTS

- Take the time to talk with and listen to the children. Ask questions and introduce topics to encourage open-ended answers and to provoke follow-up discussion and observation.

- Develop and enjoy special class hobbies, projects, and collections.

- Provide the children with lots of good books, each carefully selected to provide information and understanding related to people, places, and events around the world. Plan regular trips to the library and read-aloud sessions. Begin with books chosen to fit the children's attention span and interests and increase the complexity of materials as interest levels and listening skills mature. When selecting books, look for creativity and versatility of language usage and the sensitive portrayal of differing customs and life styles.

- Share letters, lists, stories, poems, songs, slogans, jokes, and puns to help develop a sense of humor and an awareness of time and space beyond the immediate community.

- Encourage group projects. Build with wood and nails, paint and sculpt — all of these things encourage questioning, brain flexing, and the sharing of ideas.

# HOUSEKEEPING CENTER

Set aside one corner of the classroom for a housekeeping center. Arrange the daily schedule to allow time for the children to use the center for both planned activities and free time fun. Introduce new objects and projects on a regular basis to maintain interest. For example, create a holiday or seasonal focus in the center at special times of the year, place math activities in the center at appropriate times, and emphasize creative drama, cooking, and literature at other times. First and foremost, carefully plan the center to allow for free-play, group interaction, and individual exploration.

I am special.

I am a _____ .

I have _____ hair.

I have _____ eyes.

Here is a picture of how I look.

I am _____ years old.

Next year I will be _____ .

Here is a picture of the present I would like.

Cut and paste the correct number of candles on the cake to show how old you will be on your next birthday.

Here is a picture of something my friend and I like to do together.

# This is a picture of how my home looks.

There are _____ people in my family.

Here is a picture of my family.

# ASKING GOOD QUESTIONS

The ability to formulate and verbalize good questions is essential for the young child to acquire specific information, clarify ideas or impressions, and help develop important concepts. Children especially need help in developing the skills necessary to ask good, clear questions to help them in their first learning experiences. Many children have actually been denied much-needed help simply because their questions were poorly worded or irrelevant. For this reason, it is important that a child be given an opportunity to learn to develop good questioning skills in a non-threatening environment.

## THINGS TO DO TO HELP CHILDREN ASK GOOD QUESTIONS

- Encourage the children to think through their questions before asking them and to rephrase the questions in order to gain the desired information. This takes time and patience, but the lasting results make it well worth the effort.

- Ask meaningful questions after reading a story or watching a TV program. Tell the children in advance that you will be asking questions. Allow the children to formulate and ask you questions about the same experience.

- Try to determine the intent of the child's questioning. Are questions formulated to actually gain information or are they used as attention-getting devices? If the latter is true, try to determine why attention is sought and work out ways to channel this need in a more positive direction.

- Give prompt and well thought out answers to the children's questions. Avoid answers that are too open-ended or that are beyond the children's experiential frame of reference.

- Provide a role model by asking interesting, relevant, and clearly stated questions for the children to answer.

# THINGS TO DO TO HELP CHILDREN DEVELOP POSITIVE ATTITUDES TOWARD SCHOOL

- Read the story on the following page to the class.
  Discuss:
      Why did Billy cry?
      Did you feel a little bit like crying on your first day of school? Why?
      Why did Billy stop crying? Was it because he made friends and found things to do?
      Have you made friends?
      What fun things have you found to do?
- Make a list on a chart or the chalkboard of things children like about school. Spread a big sheet of butcher paper on the floor and provide time for each child to draw a picture of the thing he or she likes most about school. Add a caption to the mural and hang it in the room to be admired.
- Prepare an "apple from the teacher" bulletin board display to feature a surprise of the day. Make a big apple tree with red construction paper apples to be turned over (one each morning) to determine the surprise of the day. (Examples: extra play period, popcorn party, finger painting, music time, making bookmarks to take home.)

# BILLY GOES TO SCHOOL
## *A Read-Aloud Story*

Billy didn't want to go to school. He wasn't afraid to go to school; he just wanted to stay home and play with his baby brother.

Billy thought that the other kids might think his hair looked funny, or that he might be the only boy in the class who couldn't write his whole name, or hit a ball, or run fast. He thought all of the other kids might have nicer clothes or neater book bags.

On the first day of school, Billy cried when he told his dad good-bye. He cried when he told his teacher hello. He cried at playtime. He cried in the lunchroom. He cried all during math and while the teacher was reading a story for the other children to act out. When Billy was leaving at the end of the day, he wiped a tear from his cheek as the teacher said, "See you tomorrow, Billy — I'm glad you're in our room."

On the second day of school, Billy cried when his mother gave him his lunch box. He was crying when he walked into the classroom, but he almost smiled when a girl behind him said, "Billy, I really like your curly hair." At playtime he was so busy wiping his nose that he scarcely heard the boy on the playground say, "Billy, please play on my team." Actually, Billy cried a good bit on the second day of school.

On the third day of school, Billy waved good-bye to his baby brother and said, "See you after school." He wrinkled his nose and fished out his handkerchief to get ready to cry. Just then he remembered that today was the day he'd promised to sit beside Johnny. The teacher had said there would be a surprise at group time today, and after that would come the free-play bell. He also had a shiny shell in his pocket for show-and-tell. On the third day of school, there just wasn't much time to cry.

On the fourth day of school, Billy said, "Bye, Dad," as he ran out the door. After that, Billy was so busy at school that he forgot all about crying.

# Here is a picture of my school.

There are _____ boys in my class.
There are _____ girls in my class.

# THINGS TO DO TO HELP CHILDREN
# LEARN WITH FAMILIAR OBJECTS

## SHOE

- Discuss different types of shoes and why different people wear the kinds of shoes they do.

- Ask children to look for pictures of different types of shoes in magazines and newspapers. Tell each child to select one picture to bring to class to tell what he or she thinks the person who wears the shoes looks like and does. Paste all of the pictures on a large piece of paper to create a collage for the bulletin board.

- Reproduce a copy of the shoe pattern for each child. Ask the children to imagine that the shoe is one of a pair of magic shoes which makes it possible for their feet to take them anywhere they want to go and to do anything they want to do. Have the children draw pictures of where they would like to go and what they would like to do if they had the matching shoe.

- Have all the children take off their shoes and place them in a line. Have fun guessing which shoes belong to which people.

- Read or tell the story "The Shoemaker and the Elves." Ask the children:
  - ... What kind of shoes do you think the elves made?
  - ... Who do you think bought the shoes?
  - ... How do you think the shoemaker and his wife felt when they awoke to find all of the shoes finished?
  - ... How do you think the elves felt?
  - ... Do you think the elves might have done other kinds of work to surprise other people who were in trouble? If so, what kind of work do you think they did?

- Make up and act out a story about another working person who was helped by the elves (a farmer, a baker, a tailor, a writer, etc.).

- Work with the concepts of left and right: left shoe, right shoe, left hand, right hand.

- Use the shoe pattern to cut a piece of tagboard. Punch holes where indicated, place a shoelace in the two bottom holes, and store the shoe in a Manila envelope. Children can lace and/or tie the shoe.

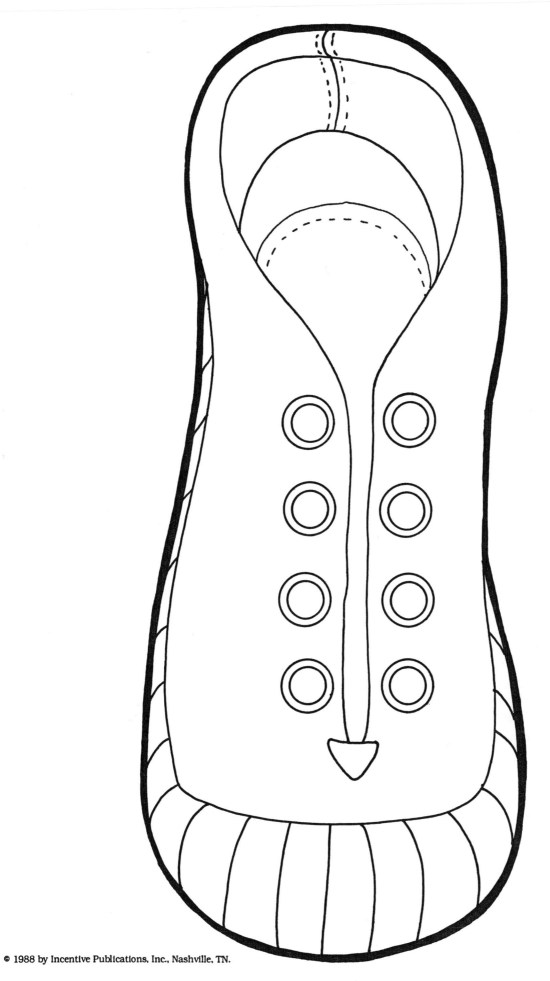

# TELEPHONE

- Make a telephone directory of names and telephone numbers of the children in the class. First, write the list on the chalkboard and let children supply their own numbers verbally. Then make a list for each child. Assist the children in stapling their directories together and decorating them with construction paper covers. Send the directories home for year-long use as a classroom directory.

- Provide telephones (made from the pattern) for all of the children. Assist each child in writing his or her own number on the phone. Continue assisting the children until they can write their numbers independently.

- Assist children in memorizing —
  ... parents' numbers at work
  ... number of someone to call if parents cannot be reached
  ... emergency numbers such as police and fire departments

- Use toy telephones for children to have make-believe conversations with each other.
  Stress telephone courtesy —
  ... identifying oneself at the beginning of the conversation
  ... beginning with a friendly greeting
  ... having polite conversation; saying "please" and "thank you"
  ... being brief
  ... never playing with the phone
  ... saying "good-bye" and making sure the receiver is not left off the hook after the conversation is over

- Bring both a push button phone and a rotary dial phone to class for the children to examine. Explain the differences in the two kinds of phones in simple terms. Allow the children to practice dialing their home numbers on both phones.

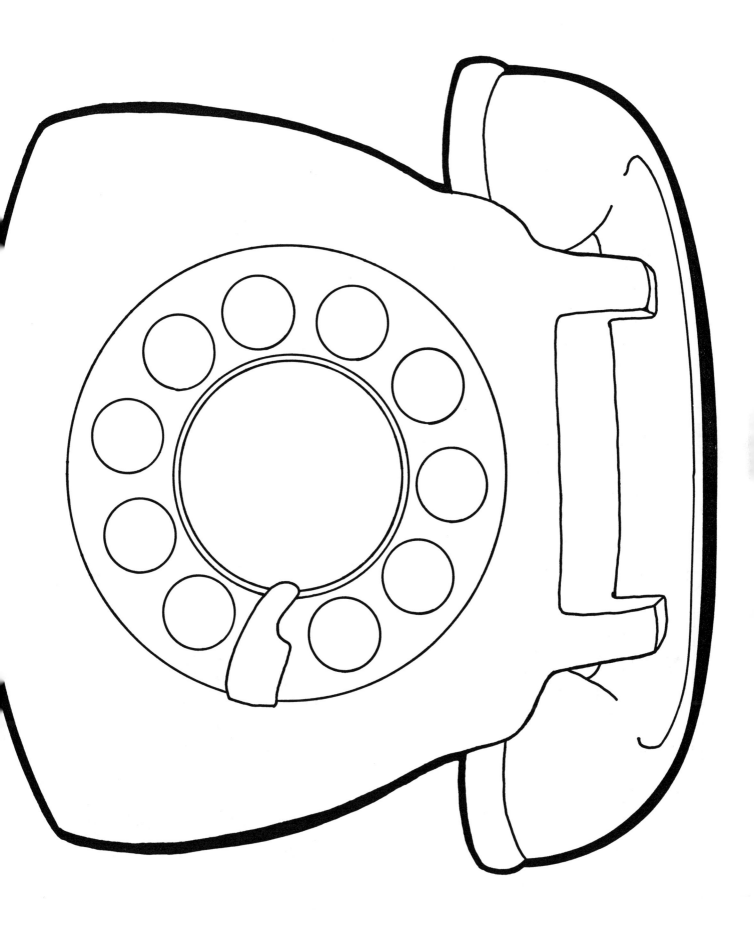

# TEDDY BEARS

- To help bridge the gap between home and school, stage a teddy bear parade. Ask each child to bring his or her favorite teddy bear (or other stuffed animal) to school. Line the bears along the chalk ledge or on a table. During the day children can discuss whose bear is whose.

- Read or tell stories about Winnie-the-Pooh, Paddington, "The Three Bears," etc. Arrange picture books on the library table with pictures of all kinds of teddy bears as well as live bears.

- Reproduce the teddy bear pattern for each child to color and cut out. Older children may write a simple sentence about the teddy bear parade.

- Serve peanut butter and honey on apple wedges as a snack.

  Mix equal parts peanut butter and honey in a big bowl. Throw in a handful of raisins. Provide a wooden spoon and allow each child to have a turn stirring. Set out apple wedges and several plastic spreaders so that each child can spread his or her own.

- Make parade awards from blue construction paper for each bear to wear home.

## YOU JUST BEARLY MISSED

### KEEP TRYING! I KNOW YOU CAN DO IT

 # HOLIDAYS

Young children love celebrations, traditions, and special times. Four, five, and six-year-olds relate to and identify quickly with merrymaking. Holiday celebrations hold mystery and intrigue for the very young who are ready to join the festivities with abandon and sincerity.

Horizons are broadened, experiential bases are stretched, and language readiness skills are developed as the young child learns about commonly celebrated holidays. As various holiday customs are explored, the child learns that while people around the world share many similar views and traditions, each person and group of people are unique and, to a certain extent, are influenced by history and environment.

## THINGS TO DO TO HELP
## CHILDREN LEARN ABOUT HOLIDAYS

- Help the children identify personally with the history and traditions surrounding family and community holidays.

- Plan special celebrations for familiar holidays (keep the plans simple and realistic — remember, the goal is for the children to participate, not to be frustrated spectators).

- Help the children make small holiday remembrances for family and friends such as ornaments or baked goods.

- Add new words and phrases to the vocabulary associated with the holidays.

- Share holidays of the past (your childhood or your grandparents' holiday memories) and discuss ways customs have changed.

- Tell or read stories of holidays celebrated by different cultural or religious groups to help build multi-cultural understanding. Act out some of the stories using improvised props and/or costumes to reinforce concepts.

# A CELEBRATION TREE

Anchor a large tree branch in a clay pot and use it to hold an ever-changing array of creative projects!

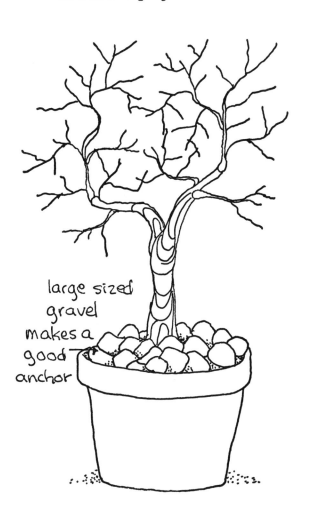

large sized gravel makes a good anchor

gather tightly with bread wrapper ties

- Make big, fat, paper bag pumpkins — and skinny ones, too! Stuff small paper bags with newspaper and then paint them.

- Ghosts are on the prowl! Drape lollipops with tissues, tie them with string, and decorate them with markers.

- Cut red, brown, and gold autumn leaves from construction paper — or spatter paintings.

spatter painted sheet

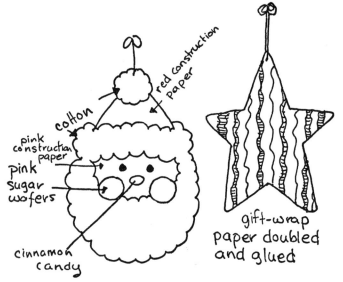

cotton

red construction paper

pink construction paper

pink sugar wafers

cinnamon candy

gift-wrap paper doubled and glued

- Design and create Christmas ornaments — stars, trees, or Santas — concocted with goodies from the scrap box, paper, scissors, crayons, glue, glitter, and lots of imagination!

poke a hole in the middle of a cup thread yarn through & knot. For added effect you may want to tie on a small jingle bell.

- Silver bells to ring in the new year are a snap with tiny paper cups, aluminum foil, and yarn for stringing.

to MY BEST FRIEND

I LoVE YoU MaMA

- Use red construction paper hearts and paper doilies to make Valentine's Day greetings . . .

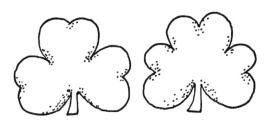

- . . . and green shamrocks to celebrate Saint Patrick's Day, of course!

- Birds, flowers, butterflies, and bumblebees are perfect for celebrating spring.

make a puppet from a glove

pin a paper face to an old hat

nut cup with yarn handle for a tiny basket

yarn & ribbon bows

- Wrap up the year with one-of-a-kind, never-thought-of-before creations made from all of the splendid odds and ends left in the scrap box, the good junk collections, and "not claimed" items from the lost and found shelf.

Color and cut out the finger puppets.
Tape them together as shown and make up a Halloween play!

# HOLIDAY RECIPES

## PUMPKIN SEEDS

1 Pumpkin

Toast pumpkin seeds!  (Great for Halloween.)
Cut off pumpkin top and scoop out pulp and
seeds. Separate seeds from pulp and place
seeds in a colander. Rinse seeds under
cold water and pat dry.
Spread seeds on cookie
sheet and bake at 400°
for about 30 minutes.
Stir seeds frequently.
Put warm seeds in a
bowl and toss with melted butter and salt. Eat
the toasted seeds at a Halloween Party!

## CHAROSES

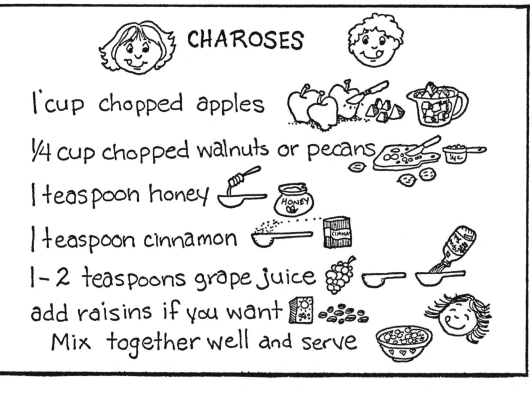

1 cup chopped apples

1/4 cup chopped walnuts or pecans

1 teaspoon honey

1 teaspoon cinnamon

1-2 teaspoons grape juice

add raisins if you want

   Mix together well and serve

Here is a picture of something I am especially thankful for.

Draw the missing parts for the toys in the stocking.
Add a toy that you would like to find in your stocking.
Color the toys.

**Holiday awareness**
© 1988 by Incentive Publications, Inc., Nashville, TN.

# FIELD TRIPS

Human development authorities agree that nothing takes the place of hands-on experiences for the young child. The most significant learning occurs through exposure to and direct contact with real people, places, and things. Carefully planned field trips provide the opportunities for children to feel, smell, touch, and taste, and to internalize social and environmental concepts at their own levels of understanding. For example, it is fine to show pictures and read stories about how milk gets from the cow to the breakfast table, but a trip to the farm allows the child to touch the cow, to observe the cow being milked, and to form a new understanding of the balance of nature.

The important thing to remember when planning educational field trips is that they must be in keeping with the child's intellectual development and within both the child's and the adult's physical and emotional stamina. A little careful planning goes a long way to insure that everyone gets the most from the trip.

- Involve the children as much as possible in selecting the site to visit and in making the plans (sometimes the planning has more educational value than the trip).

- Read and talk about the place to be visited while the trip is being planned.

- Show pictures of the place or a similar setting if additional reinforcement is needed.

- Plan to dress comfortably for the trip and to take along supplies (this includes food and drinks if they will not be readily available -- checking in advance can save a lot of misery).

- Take a camera along if you can. (One snapshot is worth a thousand words when it comes to memory making.)

- Take time immediately after the trip for the follow-up discussion. (What did we learn? Was the trip worthwhile? Did we find answers for our questions? What can we do now to learn more?)

**Take Field Trips To ...**

- **a farm** — allow time for the children to observe animals in the pasture or barnyard, to note differences in appearances and behaviors of adult and young animals, to use appropriate vocabulary (cow-calf, sheep-lamb, etc.), to identify products associated with different animals (chicken-eggs, cow-milk, sheep-wool, etc.);

  observe, feel, smell and, if appropriate, taste different produce; observe growing patterns and associate products from various plants (cotton-clothing, wheat-flour to make bread and cookies, etc.);

  observe and learn the uses of various machines and tools on the farm (plow to turn the soil for planting, rake to gather the hay, etc.);

  talk to members of the farm family to learn how each contributes to the farm life style.

- **a junkyard or garbage dump** to learn about man's use and misuse of our natural resources.

- **a bakery, cannery, meat or dairy processing plant** to learn about the process of preparing and preserving food for the marketplace.

- **a lumberyard** to observe trees turned into lumber for commercial use.

- **a city sidewalk** to observe the uniquenesses of human beings of all ages, colors and persuasions.

- **a pet store, zoo, aquarium or nature museum** to observe animals, their habits, behaviors and developmental stages.

- **museums** — go as often as possible to as many different ones available to you — plan carefully, too, so that the purpose of the trip is in keeping with the children's readiness to learn.

- **the park, forest, fields, roadsides, mountains, valleys and seashore** to help the children experience nature in all of its splendor.

# THINGS TO DO TO HELP CHILDREN
# LEARN ABOUT SAFETY

Sponsor a school safety week.

- Ask a different community helper to visit the class each day of the week (nurse or doctor, firefighter, police officer, etc.). Arrange to visit the work places of community helpers who are unable to come to school.

- Help the children work together to make road signs and traffic lights using construction paper, poster board, craft sticks, crayons and markers, and other art supplies. Discuss the purpose and use of each sign. Invent games using the signs which the children may play at school or at home (using homemade signs) to become familiar with the signs and their importance.

- Make a list of safety rules using a large poster board and colorful markers. Lead a creative safety discussion in which each rule is covered. Encourage children to contribute to the discussion by talking about personal experiences, by adding other important safety rules to the list, and by asking questions.

- Provide the children with art materials to make poison warnings for products containing harmful chemicals or substances. Send a letter home with each child asking parents to tape the warning labels to harmful household products.

- Ask the school principal to schedule a fire drill for one day of the safety week. After the drill, have the children sit in a circle and discuss what happened. Talk about what was good about the drill, what should not have happened, and what things should have taken place. Lead a discussion about general safety procedures.

- Take the children on a safety walk. Point out safety rules such as crossing streets properly, staying on sidewalks, observing traffic, staying together, avoiding strange animals, noticing landmarks, etc. Discuss the walk after returning to the classroom.

```
┌─────────────────────────────────────────────────────────┐
│                                                         │
│ ─ ─ ─ ─ ─ ─ ─ ─ ─ ─ ─ ─ ─ ─ ─ ─ ─ ─ ─ ─ ─ ─ ─ ─ ─ ─ ─ │
│                                                         │
│                                                         │
└─────────────────────────────────────────────────────────┘
```

knows these important safety rules and has earned this
   special badge.

☐   I know my full name, address and telephone number.
☐   I never get in a car or leave with anyone I do not know.
☐   If someone I do not know tries to take me away, I will yell
       loudly.
☐   I never accept treats and presents from strangers.
☐   I never wander away from the group when I am playing
       outside.

**Safety awareness**
© 1988 by Incentive Publications, Inc., Nashville, TN.

Draw a line from each hat to its owner.

Can you tell what each community helper does?

Cut the puzzle pieces apart along the dotted lines.
Ask children to match the community helpers to the
   proper tools.
The puzzle pieces may also be backed with felt for use
   as an independent felt board activity.

# Whatever Shall I Be?

When I grow up, I'd like to be
The captain of a ship at sea,
Or pilot jets to far away
And bring them back another day.

Perhaps I'd rather tell the news
And do important interviews,
Write songs or books or poems or plays
Or dance in beautiful ballets.

I could be a detective who catches thieves
Or a gardener fine who rakes great piles of leaves,
A plumber, a drummer, a daring sky diver,
A mayor, bricklayer or taxicab driver . . .

An astronaut brave who rockets so high
Or a master chef who is known for his pie,
A florist, a seamstress, a doctor, a farmer,
A basketball player or a famous snake charmer.
How will I decide just what I will be?
There are so many jobs . . . which one is for me?
Someday I will know, and I'll choose my own,
But today I'll just dream what I'll be when I'm grown.

One day I will be all grown up.
Here is a picture of what I will do then.

# BOOKS TO HELP CHILDREN DEVELOP SOCIAL AWARENESS AND SELF-CONCEPT

Delaney, Ned. **Bert and Barney.** Boston: Houghton Mifflin.
> *A frog named Bert and his best friend Barney the alligator go their separate ways after a disagreement and are brought together again after a near disaster.*

Felt, Sue. **Rosa-Too-Little.** New York: Doubleday.
> *A little girl named Rosa experiences joy and pride after she finally learns to write her name and thus receive a library card of her very own.*

Flack, Marjorie. **The Story About Ping.** New York: Penguin Books.
> *Ping ventures into the world and encounters loneliness and fear but also finds friends and new experiences. Children relate warmly to Ping's desires for independence and dependence.*

Kellogg, Steven. **Can I Keep Him?** New York: Dial Press.
> *A mother says no to her little boy who wants to keep one pet after another (real, imaginary, and human). The problem is finally solved by a new friend.*

Kraus, Robert. **Leo the Late Bloomer.** New York: Windmill Books.
> *A small tiger reassures young learners that it is all right to learn to read, write, and do other things at your own rate.*

Leaf, Munro. **Ferdinand the Bull.** New York: Viking Press.
> *This story about a bull who chooses to be himself in every way reinforces the concept of respect for individualism in a most delightful manner.*

Lionni, Leo. **Swimmy.** New York: Pantheon Books.
> *A little fish who looks and thinks differently from other fish helps children see that differences are not only acceptable but are just fine.*

Stren, Patti. **Hug Me.** New York: Harper & Row.
> *This funny little story with simple text and drawings reminds youngsters that sometimes everyone needs a hug.*

Udry, Janice May. **Let's Be Enemies.** New York: Harper & Row.
> *This story about the ups and downs of friendship helps children develop an understanding of themselves and others.*

Viorst, Judith. **Alexander and the Terrible, Horrible, No Good, Very Bad Day.** New York: Atheneum.
> *All children (and adults, as well) can relate to Alexander's feelings as he experiences a day in which absolutely nothing goes right.*

Zolotow, Charlotte. **William's Doll.** New York: Harper & Row.
> *A little boy named William really wants a doll. His sensitive grandmother steps in to help handle this desire which no one else understands.*

# LANGUAGE

# AUDIO AND VISUAL RECEPTION AND COMPREHENSION

Young children tend to learn language skills more readily and with more of a positive attitude when they can directly associate planned learning activities with personal experiences. Children who are spoken to, listened to, and allowed to question and experiment will have a real head start in learning to read and write. These are the children who will be able to relate to reading, writing, and reasoning as logical steps in their normal development.

It is a fact that children learn more from what they see, hear, and feel than from what they are told. Young children are extremely sensitive to and strongly influenced by their physical environment. Readiness for reading and writing is developed as children are encouraged to interpret and talk about pictures, to observe and analyze social situations, and to be sensitive to body language and facial expressions. Providing the opportunity for children to share real life experiences as well as to talk about books and ideas as a regular part of the day will encourage intellectual curiosity and will provide readiness for structured activities.

Once the readiness stage is determined, the child needs consistent guidance in developing the auditory and visual skills necessary for building a firm foundation for reading and writing success. The checklists on the following pages may be used for evaluation and record keeping related to the child's mastery of readiness skills as reflected in independent projects or structured pencil and paper activities.

The "Things To Do" section following each checklist is composed of quick and easy activities and projects that will help teach and reinforce skills and concepts in a non-threatening and fun setting. Although each of the accompanying work sheets is skill-based, all have been designed around topics of high interest to young children and should be presented in a relaxed and enjoyable environment. When presenting one of these activities it is important to remember to plan so that each child is allowed to progress at an individual rate, completely free of competition with other children.

# MOTOR SKILLS CHECKLIST

### Gross Motor Skills
- ☐ is able to recognize body parts
- ☐ is able to balance
- ☐ is able to jump
- ☐ is able to hop
- ☐ is able to skip
- ☐ is able to throw
- ☐ is able to catch
- ☐ is able to ride a tricycle
- ☐ is able to bounce a ball
- ☐ is able to kick a ball
- ☐ is able to move rhythmically to music

### Fine Eye-Hand Motor Skills
- ☐ is able to paste
- ☐ is able to cut
- ☐ is able to trace a drawn pattern
- ☐ is able to copy pegboard patterns
- ☐ is able to copy shapes (square, circle, triangle, rectangle, cross, diamond)
- ☐ is able to reproduce simple designs (lined and shaded)
- ☐ is able to work puzzles
- ☐ is able to demonstrate "left to right" eye and hand movements when performing writing tasks

# THINGS TO DO TO HELP CHILDREN DEVELOP MOTOR SKILLS

- Puzzles, dot-to-dot activities and coloring are good for fine and gross muscle control but not for creative endeavors. Use puzzles, dot-to-dot activities and coloring books to strengthen each child's ability to trace and color within a restricted area.

- Form a circle. Bounce a ball to one child at a time. Have the child catch the ball and bounce it back.

- Practice sewing using a large needlepoint needle or one with a blunt point. Have the children learn to thread the needle with knitting yarn. Use sewing cards (which can be purchased) or draw your own design on lightweight cardboard. Punch holes along the lines of the design and have the children sew the design with the needle and thread.

- Have the children practice making the upper-case letters between the lines of large-lined paper.

- Have the children practice tracing around household objects such as cans, spoons, square containers, keys, recipe cards, or scissors. Make a dotted pattern of these items on a piece of paper. Then the children may follow and trace over these dotted patterns.

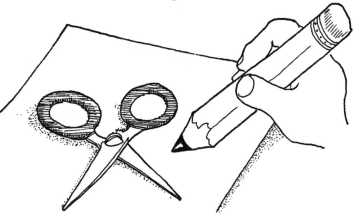

- Use a balance beam or a chalk line drawn on the floor for children to practice walking along a straight line for three feet, six feet, etc. Extend the distance until 10 to 15 feet can be mastered.

## Visual Receptive and Comprehension Skills Checklist

- ☐ understands the use of objects (categorization)
- ☐ knows colors
- ☐ knows shapes
- ☐ knows the letters in his name
- ☐ demonstrates understanding of size differences
- ☐ can identify the concepts of top, middle, bottom, front and back
- ☐ can match letters in the alphabet (upper and lower case)
- ☐ can recognize his written name
- ☐ can reproduce visual sequential patterns
- ☐ can categorize objects by matching
- ☐ can recognize common labels and symbols
- ☐ can recognize visual similarities
- ☐ can recognize visual differences
- ☐ can interpret pictures

## Auditory Receptive and Comprehension Skills Checklist

- ☐ can recognize environmental sounds
- ☐ can discriminate sound similarities and differences
- ☐ can discriminate beginning word sounds
- ☐ can discriminate middle word sounds
- ☐ can discriminate ending word sounds
- ☐ can rhyme words
- ☐ can blend sounds into words
- ☐ can repeat a sequence of five words
- ☐ can identify letters of the alphabet by name
- ☐ can verbally count sequentially from one to ten
- ☐ can count ten objects
- ☐ can identify the concepts of first, second and third
- ☐ can use complete sentences
- ☐ can answer questions
- ☐ can follow directions
- ☐ can listen to short stories or group discussions without restlessness
- ☐ can repeat simple nursery rhymes
- ☐ can retell a short story (including plot, main ideas and characters)
- ☐ understands analogies
- ☐ uses a functional vocabulary

# THINGS TO DO TO HELP CHILDREN DEVELOP VISUAL PERCEPTION

- Place simple geometric shapes on a table. Have the children pick out the shapes that are the same size, shape or color.

- Buy two identical magazines. Cut out brightly colored pictures from one. Have the children find and cut out the same pictures from the other magazine.

  Tear identical full-page, full-color pictures from the magazines. Paste one picture on a Manila envelope. Cut the other picture into simple puzzle pieces. Store the puzzle pieces in the Manila envelope. Have the children use the picture on the envelope as a model to work the puzzle.

- Cut out pictures of animals, flowers, or toys from one magazine. Outline the shapes of these items on a piece of paper. Have the children find and cut out from the second magazine items that will match the outline shapes. Store the originals in an envelope to use as a reference.

- Choose a can of food from a collection on a table. Give it to the child and let him or her select an identical can from the table.
- Build a pattern on a pegboard and have the child reproduce it.

- Let each child choose from a collection three shirts or three socks that are alike in some way. They may all have stripes, solids, checks, similar designs, etc.

55

# THINGS TO DO TO HELP
# CHILDREN DEVELOP AUDITORY PERCEPTION

- Strengthen sequential memory through repetition. Clap your hands using a distinct pattern. Ask the children to reproduce the pattern.

- Give the children sample sequences to remember and repeat. For example:

  — cap, shoes, socks
  — eight, four, two
  — paper, fruit, flower
  — red, yellow, blue
  — game, bag, desk
  — pen, roof, carton

- Give the children sample sentences to repeat, such as:

  — Jerry reads books about knights and dragons.
  — April plays games and reads books.
  — My brother took me to the video shop and we rented twenty-six cartoons.
  — Grandmother knitted a sweater that was red, blue and pink.

- Choose a word such as "goat" and ask the children to tell you some rhyming words.

- Ask the children to name words which share the same beginning sound (i.e. ball, boat, big, etc.).

- Ask the children to draw pictures that begin or end with the same sound as "horse."

- Say two words that rhyme and one that does not. Have the children tell you which word does not rhyme and then say aloud other rhyming words.

- Using a record player or tape recorder, have the children skip or dance to the music and sit down when the music stops. (This helps in distinguishing sounds and in following directions.)

- Blindfold the children and have them sit in chairs. Make sounds from different locations in the room. Ask the children to point in the direction of each sound.

- Ask the children to clap, stomp, march, sway, dance, snap, jump, hop, or any combination of these to the rhythm of a musical accompaniment.

# RHYMING WORDS

Using rhyming words and word patterns such as nursery rhymes, jump rope jingles, sing-alongs, and clapping games provides reinforcement for both auditory and word recognition development. One of the best things about activities of this nature is that they integrate play and learning in a delightful manner, allowing children to abandon themselves freely to the learning situation.

Each group of children will enjoy building a collection of special favorites and making up original ones of their own.

## JUMP ROPE JINGLES

### TEDDY BEAR

Teddy Bear, Teddy Bear, turn around,
Teddy Bear, Teddy Bear, touch the ground,
Teddy Bear, Teddy Bear, show your shoe,
Teddy Bear, Teddy Bear, that will do!

Teddy Bear, Teddy Bear, go upstairs,
Teddy Bear, Teddy Bear, say your prayers,
Teddy Bear, Teddy Bear, switch off the light,
Teddy Bear, Teddy Bear, say good-night.

### I LOVE COFFEE

I love coffee,
I love tea,
I want (child's name)
to come in with me.

### POLLY PUT THE KETTLE ON

Polly put the kettle on
And have a cup of tea,
In comes (child's name)
And goes out with me.

### HONEY AND RICE, SAY IT TWICE

Bread and butter,
Sugar and spice,
Honey and rice,
Say it twice,
One, two, three...(count as you jump)

# CLAPPING GAMES

## WHO STOLE THE COOKIES FROM THE COOKIE JAR?

Group: Who stole the cookies from the cookie jar?
(Child's name) stole the cookies from the cookie jar.
Who me?
Group: Yes, you!
Not me!
Group: Then who?
(Child's name) stole the cookies from the cookie jar. (Name new child.)
Who me?
Group: Yes, you!
Not me!
Group: Then, who?
(Continue in this way.)

The group sits in a circle and decides whose name will be called first. Then the group chants in rhythm while slapping knees first and then clapping hands.

## BABY DOLL

Baby Doll, Baby Doll, have you heard?
Papa's gonna buy me a mockingbird.
*alternate clapping hands and knees*

If that mockingbird don't sing,
Papa's gonna buy me a diamond ring.
*alternate clapping hands and thighs*

If that diamond ring don't shine,
Papa's gonna buy me a fishing line.
*alternate clapping hands and chest*

Baby Doll, Baby Doll, where you been?
Around the world and I'm going again.
*alternate clapping hands and shoulders*

The group sits in a circle and claps.

# FOLLOWING DIRECTIONS

Young children will profit from being taught to listen to and follow simple verbal instructions in an orderly and organized manner. Adjustment to structured learning situations is much easier for the child who is provided with many opportunities to carry out directed activities in everyday settings. For example, you might give these instructions: "Bring me two books, one pencil and a magazine. Color this picture with your red, green and blue crayons. Touch your head, your chest, and then your knee." Another good way to provide experience in following directions is to give instructions for seatwork activities such as directing the children to draw a red circle, a green square, and an orange triangle.

## Teacher's Checklist For Helping Young Children Learn To Listen To And Follow Directions

☐ Make sure that the children are ready to listen to and follow the directions before you give them.

☐ Use a quiet, firm voice when giving directions.

☐ Help the children analyze, clarify, and understand any sequence involved and develop a workable plan for completing the instructions.

☐ Tell the children that the directions will be given only once. If the directions are unclear, questions should be asked immediately to clarify any confusion.

☐ Be kind and considerate, yet firm. The children know if you mean what you say.

☐ Use paper and pencil activities to help the children move from following verbal directions to following written directions.

☐ Accept and reward the children's efforts with praise and positive encouragement. Avoid criticism or pressure.

☐ Give prompt and meaningful answers to questions.

☐ Include the children in adult conversations at a level that is realistic and meaningful.

☐ Encourage verbal expression of ideas and concepts.

# STORYTELLING

It is never too early to begin reading or telling stories to children. Educators agree that telling stories is one of the most effective methods for developing early language skills and for monitoring auditory and perception skills progress.

Listening skills are taught, not caught, so it is important to begin with short stories having few characters, uncluttered settings, and simple plots. As children's attention spans and comprehension levels increase, stories may be selected accordingly.

Follow-up is an important part of story time, but it should be kept short, to the point, and unpressured. There are better times for direct teaching of basic skills. Remember, this is not a time for lecturing, generalizing, or disciplining. Story time is a magic time, worthy of its own special place.

The following list of stories includes many all-time favorites, each one capable of holding a child as spellbound now as the first time it was told.

**Marco Comes Late.** Dr. Seuss.
> —a fun, rhyming story that tells the tale of a young boy's excuse for being late to school.

**Ask Mr. Bear.** Marjorie Flack.
> —Danny asks several different animals about what he should give his mother for her birthday, and Mr. Bear has just the answer.

**The Cobbler's Tale.** Elizabeth Orton Jones.
> —the story of how a wise old cat figures out how to make the king's shoe comfortable.

**Gingham Lena.** Emma L. Brock.
> —a young girl searches high and low for her doll Brin Hilda, who is missing.

**Horton and the Kwuggerbug.** Dr. Seuss.
> —the tale of how the Kwuggerbug leads Horton the elephant to the Beezlenut tree, and the deal they make about the nuts.

**Little Duckling Tries His Voice.** Marjorie La Fleur.
> —Little Duckling journeys into the wide world to discover the way he would like to talk.

**A Tragic Story.** William Makepeace Thackeray.
> —the poetic story of a sage's attempt to have his pigtail hang in front of him rather than behind him.

**A Ballad of China.** Laura E. Richards.
> —a wicked wizard steals the niece of the Empress of China until she is saved by a panther named Bill.

**The Tale of Peter Rabbit.** Beatrix Potter.
> —Peter disobeys his mother and wanders into Mr. McGregor's garden. The farmer chases him unitl Peter finally escapes and makes his way home.

**A Visit From St. Nicholas.** Clement Clarke Moore.
> —" 'Twas the night before Christmas, when all through the house . . ." begins the story of a visit from St. Nick.

**The Shoemaker and the Elves.** Jakob and Wilhelm Grimm.
> —a poor shoemaker gets help making shoes from some thoughtful elves that appear at midnight.

# Color inside the shapes.
# Trace the dotted lines.

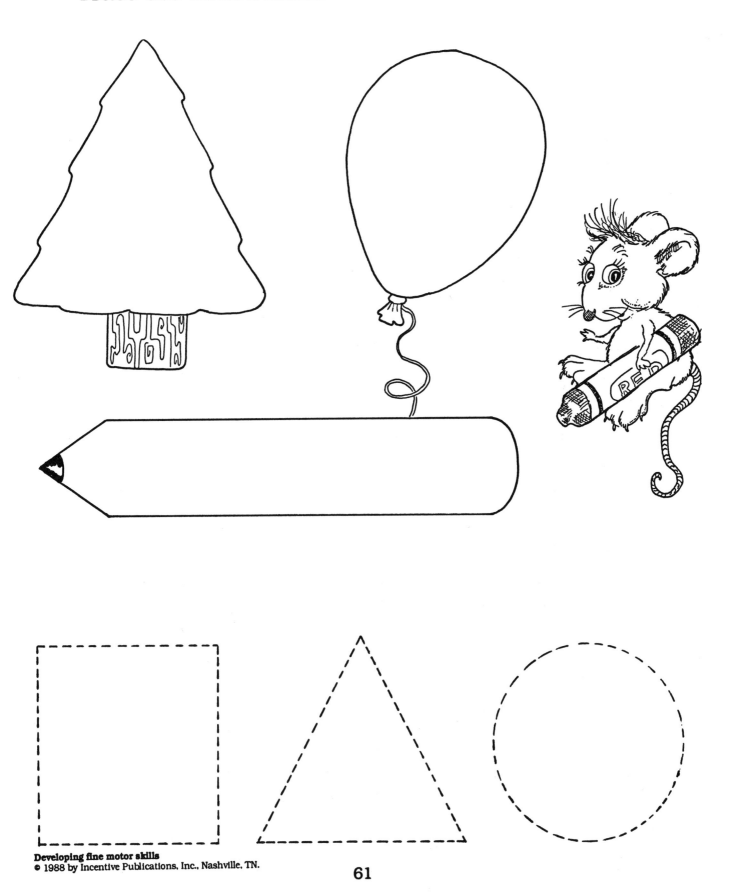

In each row, look at the picture in the first box.
Trace the picture in the second box.
Copy the picture in the last box.

**Visual motor coordination/copying**
© 1988 by Incentive Publications, Inc., Nashville, TN.

# Trace along the dotted path.

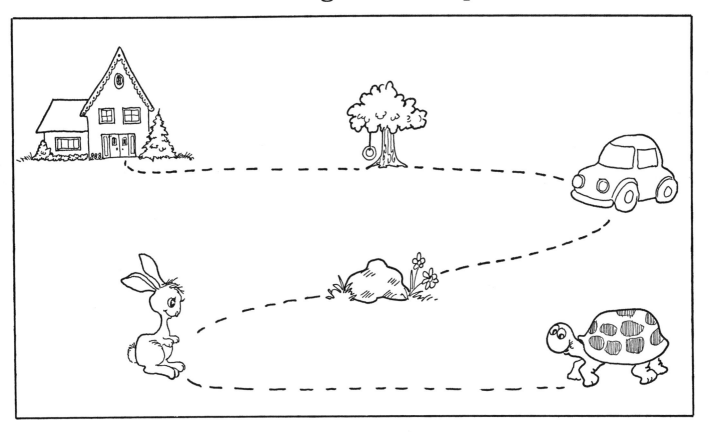

## Draw the same path below.

# Trace the lines from the animals to their homes.

Trace the lines from the boys to their toys.
Which toy would you like to have?

Something is wrong.
Find and circle the mistake in each picture.
Color everything except the mistake.

**Visual discrimination/finding mistakes**
© 1988 by Incentive Publications, Inc., Nashville, TN.

Finish drawing this truck.
Color the truck.
Make up a funny story about something that happened
   to the truck.

# Circle the animal in each group that is different. Which animal would you like to have for a pet?

Cut and paste the rhyming words.

What a funny cat.
The funny cat is so

One, two, three.
The bee is in the

fat    tree

Using rhyming words
© 1988 by Incentive Publications, Inc., Nashville, TN.

Cut and paste the correct bird to finish the riddle.
Color the picture.

I like water.
I have feathers.
My name rhymes with luck.
I am a _____ .

# BEGINNING READING AND WRITING

"I can read!" "I can write!" How thrilling it is to observe the joy and satisfaction that comes to the young child as he or she begins to unlock the mysteries of the printed page. Eyes sparkle as the child realizes for the first time that "reading is just talk written down" and that reading is not so difficult after all.

Like the development of any other set of skills, reading and writing skills are sequentially developed and interrelated. Actually, building sound language skills is analogous to the construction of a building. You must first establish a firm foundation and then check to make sure that appropriate reinforcement is provided at each stage in the building process.

If a child fails to gain a firm grasp of beginning reading skills, problems may arise that will not show up until much later. Unfortunately, these problems may become stumbling blocks that influence the child's attitude toward reading, the child's interest in learning, and consequently his or her success in school.

The sensitive teacher can help guard against this by consistently monitoring the child's oral reading progress to make sure that none of the skills necessary for reading and writing independence are being neglected. Another way is through the use of pencil and paper activities that reveal the extent to which specific skills are being mastered. The activity sheets in this book have been designed for this use. They should be presented to the child in a non-threatening manner and as a treat rather than a treatment.

Directed teaching and structured activity, as well as choice of books for free reading, should take into account the child's innate ability and unique learning style. Emphasis on drill and memorization can oftentimes do more harm than good. Remember, shoving or pushing is not in order. This very special time in a child's life is to be shared and enjoyed.

# BEGINNING READING SKILLS CHECKLIST

☐ is able to recognize all 26 letters of the alphabet

☐ is able to discriminate upper-case and lower-case letters

☐ is able to recognize alphabetical sequence

☐ is able to recognize consonant sounds

☐ is able to recognize vowel sounds

☐ is able to recognize words

☐ is able to associate words and pictures

☐ is able to associate words and ideas

☐ is able to find the main idea

☐ is able to classify materials read

☐ is able to order ideas in sequence

☐ is able to draw conclusions

☐ is able to visualize

☐ is able to recall information read

☐ is able to follow directions

## THINGS TO DO TO HELP CHILDREN DEVELOP BEGINNING READING SKILLS

• Be certain that books are associated with happy occasions and pleasant experiences.

• Read aloud as often as possible from a variety of sources geared toward the children's developmental level(s).

• Visit a library regularly as a class and provide help in the selection of books to be checked out.

• Demonstrate the turning of pages in a book from right to left and the opening of a book at the front and reading toward the back.

• Have the children play hopscotch with letters instead of numerals.

• Cut pictures from magazines, catalogs, etc., and paste them on a 4" x 8" piece of construction paper or lightweight cardboard. Punch a hole beside each picture on the edge of the cardboard. Knot a shoestring in each hole. On an additional 4" x 8" piece of cardboard, write single letters or digraphs. Punch a hole beside each letter. Match the pictures with the letters by lacing the shoestring into the holes.

- Make a flashcard for each of the consonant sounds. Ask the children to find objects that begin with the sound of each letter. Example: T—table, toy, TV; B—bowl, box, etc.

- Make alphabet cards and place them on the floor. (Exclude vowels in the beginning.) Have the child toss a bean bag and then give a word or choose something in the room with the same beginning sound as the letter on which the bag lands.

- Print a different letter on each of several envelopes. Have the children cut out pictures from magazines and catalogs that begin with the sounds the letters stand for and place the pictures in the appropriate envelopes.

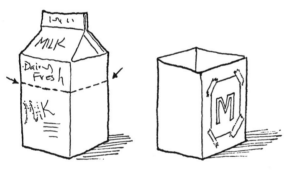

- Cut off the tops of several milk cartons about six inches from the bottom. Attach a specific letter to each carton. Have the children fill the cartons with items to match the sound on each carton.

- Have the children fold a piece of drawing paper into fourths to make a booklet. Ask the children to draw pictures of things that begin with a specific sound on each page.

- Label windows, doors, books, plants, tables, chairs, and many other concrete objects. Provide duplicate labels and ask the children to match the words to the words taped to the real objects.

- Encourage the children to dictate stories to be printed and made available for reading and re-reading. Begin with one or two-word captions for pictures, and move to longer phrases and finally to simple one-line sentences.

- Just as each child has a family, words have families, too. Choose a word and ask the children to give two other words that rhyme with that word. For example:

| boy | cow | cat |
|-----|-----|-----|
| toy | how | bat |
| joy | now | mat |

- Tie a magnet on a piece of string and attach it to a pencil or ruler. Write letters on index cards. Attach

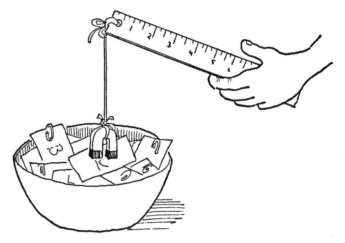

a paper clip to each card. Let a child go "fishing" in a bowl filled with the cards. After the child "catches a fish," he or she must identify the letter and the sound.

# SIGHT VOCABULARY WORDS

The words below are some that young children frequently encounter as they begin to relate to the printed word. Familiarity with these words may be reinforced by using flashcards, labeling familiar objects, playing games, and stimulating conversation.

| | |
|---|---|
| **you** | **ball** |
| **boy** | **girl** |
| **yes** | **no** |
| **I** | **me** |
| **see** | **we** |

# WRITING

Young children are naturally interested in learning to write. Often they will ask for paper and pencil and for help in writing their names, the names of their family members, and other words of importance to them. Certainly this desire should be nourished and strengthened; however, formal writing should never be pushed upon a child before readiness is demonstrated.

## THINGS TO DO TO HELP CHILDREN DEVELOP WRITING SKILLS

- Plan exercises to develop left to right and top to bottom eye movement.

- Provide large sheets of paper, properly lined tablets, and large pencils for beginning writing projects.

- Demonstrate the way in which letters are formed as you print for the children.

- Encourage the children to dictate stories from their own experiences for you to print and the children to illustrate.

- Show the children how to hold chalk, crayons and pencils correctly.

- Help the children by cheerfully finishing letters or words or by writing parts of sentences that they begin.

- Provide a model of correctly formed letters for the children to refer to as needed (don't insist on rigid conformity).

- Demonstrate how to write on lines and how to correctly space words.

- Praise all efforts and encourage interest by displaying "written work" on the bulletin board or other designated space. (The important thing at this point is to develop a love for reading and writing and to help each child feel successful.)

# Can you print your ABC's?

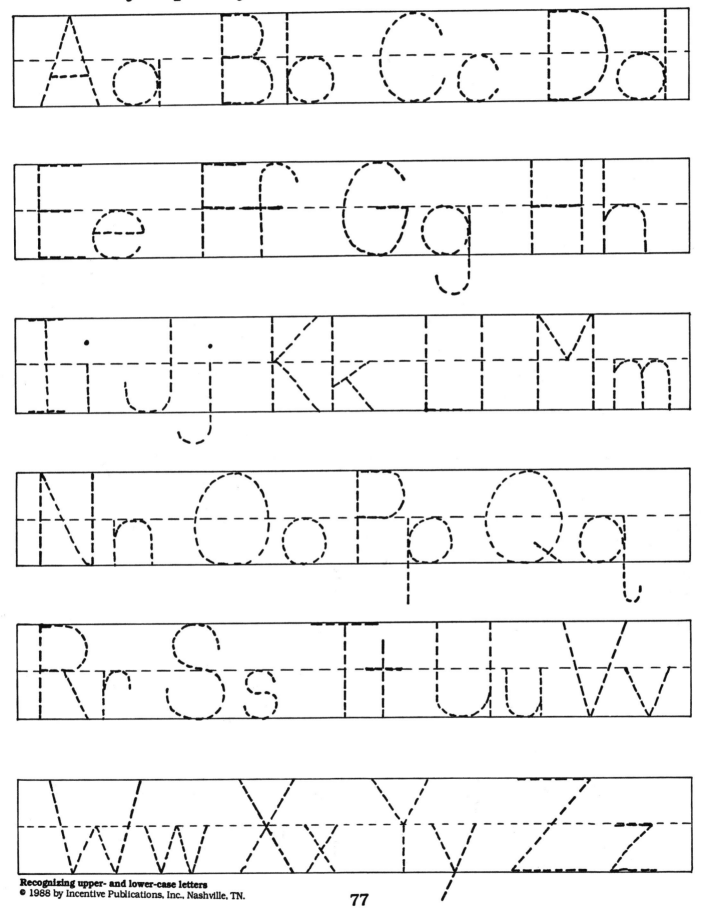

# Print the missing letters.

a ___ c ___ e ___

g ___ i ___ k

___ m ___ o ___

q ___ s ___

u ___ w ___

___ y ___

# Find and color all 26 letters of the alphabet.

Cut the puzzle pieces apart.
Ask the children to match each letter to the object that
   begins with the letter.
Have the children color each letter puzzle piece and its
   object the same color.

Cut the puzzle pieces apart.
Ask the children to match each letter to the object that
begins with that letter.
Have the children color each letter puzzle piece and its
object the same color.

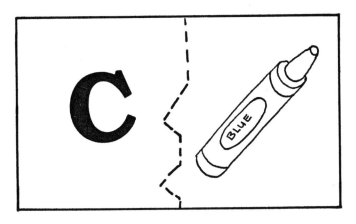

# Cut and paste the beginning vowel sound for each picture.

# Circle the picture in each balloon that does not rhyme.

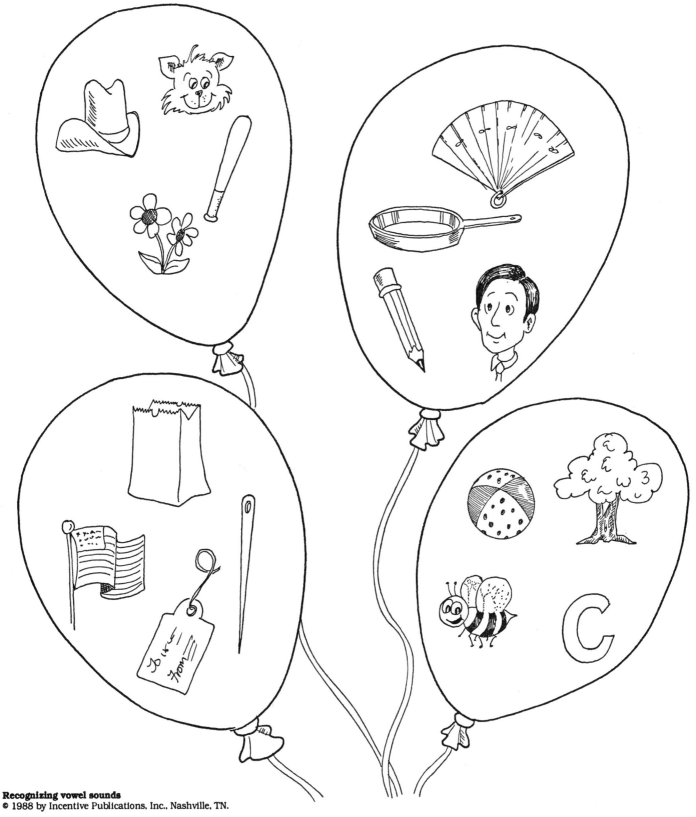

**Recognizing vowel sounds**
© 1988 by Incentive Publications, Inc., Nashville, TN.

Draw a line from each picture to the correct word.
Color the pictures.

spring

summer

fall

winter

Look at the comic strips.
Circle the best title for each one.

1. An unexpected ride.

2. The boy who wore a hat.

1. A day in the country.

2. Rain and sunshine help flowers grow.

**Finding the main idea**
© 1988 by Incentive Publications, Inc., Nashville, TN.

# Circle the picture that does not belong.

Help Nora clean out her sewing basket.
Mark out the item in each group that does not belong
   in a sewing basket.
Color the other items.

Cut out the pictures.
Paste them in the correct order to tell the story.

Little Miss Muffet
Sat on a tuffet
Eating her curds and whey.
When along came a spider
And sat down beside her
And frightened Miss Muffet away!

| | | |
|---|---|---|
| l | 2 | 3 |

# Draw a picture to show what you think happened next.

# Draw a picture to show what you think will happen next.

It was such a friendly kitten.
Danny wanted to bring it home, but he knew his mother
 would say no.
Maybe he could bring some milk outside.
Maybe he could hide the kitten in his room.
Draw a picture to show what you think happened.

**Drawing conclusions**
© 1988 by Incentive Publications, Inc., Nashville, TN.

A funny, old giant
So big and gruff,
Met a tiny, little elf
Who was not at all tough.
Said the giant to the elf,
"What brings you this way?"
And the elf was so frightened,
He didn't know what to say!

Finish the picture to show the elf.

Little Jack Horner,
Sat in a corner
Eating his Christmas pie.
He stuck in his thumb
And pulled out a plum,
And said, "What a good boy am I!"

Draw Jack's pie.

Color the house red.
Color the sun yellow.
Color the flowers blue.
Color the wagon brown.

Draw a cake on the plate.
Color the cake red.
Draw 5 candles on the cake.

**Following directions**
© 1988 by Incentive Publications, Inc., Nashville, TN.

Look at the picture.
Cover the page.
Draw the picture as you remember it.

# READING INDEPENDENCE AND SELF-EXPRESSION

For far too long, parents and teachers have been overly concerned with teaching children to read as opposed to helping them become independent readers. Certainly, none of us would disagree with the fact that teaching basic reading skills is one of the school's most important responsibilities. Most of us have observed, however, that in many instances both parents and teachers tend to lose sight of the importance of self-directed reading.

Even from the beginning reading stage, children need to be encouraged to develop both the skills and attitudes so important to reading independence. They need to be led to approach books and printed material as simply "something very special" and to look upon reading as a natural and normal part of everyday life. The child who is read to regularly and is provided with an abundance of good books and developmentally appropriate reading and writing activities will have a "head start" on becoming a lifelong reader.

Ask someone you like to read a book to you.
Ask the person to write the name of the book here.

_____

Draw a picture to show what the book is about here.

**Relating to materials read**
© 1988 by Incentive Publications, Inc., Nashville, TN.

Ask a grownup to help you write the names or draw pictures of your 3 favorite books.

Make a red star beside the one you like best of all.

Color and cut out the 2 bookmarks.
One is for you to use in your favorite book.
The other is for you to give to a friend.

Ask someone to read the rhymes aloud to you.
Then you read the rhymes for someone else to act out.

To market, to market
To buy a fat hog.
Home again, home again
Jiggety jog.

Jack be nimble,
Jack be quick,
Jack jump over the candlestick.

Little Boy Blue,
Come blow your horn,
The sheep's in the meadow,
The cow's in the corn.

Where is the boy
Who looks after the sheep?
He's under the haystack
Fast asleep.

Draw a picture to show what Little Boy Blue is dreaming of.

# Draw pictures to show what you think is in the fairy godmother's bag.

# Draw faces to show how the children feel. Tell what you think will happen next.

Here are the pickle people.
Make one grumpy and grouchy.
Give one a twinkle in his eye.
Let the last one be bashful and shy.
Now, tell a story about these characters.

# BEAUTIFUL PICTURE BOOKS
# FOR THE BEGINNING READER

Berger, Barbara. **Grandfather Twilight.** New York: Putnam.
   —soft, glowing illustrations accompany this simple story of twilight personified as a gentle grandfather.
Burton, Virginia Lee. **Katy and the Big Snow.** New York: Houghton Mifflin.
   —*little children's eyes get as big as saucers as they watch Katy, a monstrous tractor of iron and steel, rescue a big city.*
DeRegniers, B.S. **A Little House of Your Own.** New York: Harcourt, Brace and World.
   —*the author takes the reader to all the "private" little places where children might find a special hideaway.*
Ets, Marie Hall. **Play With Me.** New York: Viking Press.
   —*a little girl chases meadow creatures in search of a playmate. They all run away until she learns to sit quietly and wait. Then she is made happy by her reward.*
Gramatky, Hardie. **Little Toot.** New York: Putnam.
   —*a conceited little tugboat learns a lesson and becomes a hero.*
House, Charles. **The Biggest Mouse in the World.** New York: W.W. Norton and Co.
   —*a very small field mouse makes himself the dread of his enemies with a magic glass.*
Hyman, Trina Schart. **Rapunzel.** New York: Holiday House.
   —*graceful, detailed illustrations enhance this well-known fairy tale.*
Lifton, Betty Jean. **The Secret Seller.** New York: W.W. Norton and Co.
   —*a little boy, distressed because his friends won't tell him their secrets, comes to possess the greatest secret of them all.*
McCloskey, Robert. **Blueberries for Sal.** New York: Viking Press.
   —*a delightful tale of a little girl who meets a baby bear while hunting for blueberries.*
Sendak, Maurice. **Where the Wild Things Are.** New York: Harper and Row.
   —*a wild, playful fantasy with a perfect ending!*
Shulevitz, Uri. **Dawn.** Tacoma, Washington: Sunburst.
   —*the quiet mood set by the sun's gradual appearance over a mountain lake is shared by a father and son.*
Slobodkina, Esphyr. **Caps for Sale.** New York: W.R. Scott.
   —*a cap peddler takes a nap under a tree and wakes up to find that his caps have been taken over by a monkey business!*
VanAllsburg, Chris. **The Polar Express.** Boston: Houghton Mifflin.
   —*vibrant pastel pictures illustrate the story of a young boy's magic train ride to the North Pole.*

# GOOD BOOKS TO READ ALOUD

Hawkins, Colin, and Jacquie. **Mig The Pig.** New York: G.P. Putnam's Sons.
*Mig the Pig wears a red wig and dances a jig. This is the story of a comical pig told in simple rhyming words. Half-page flips change the beginning consonant, creating new rhyming words.*

Hertz, Ole. **Tobias Catches A Trout,** trans. Tobi Tobias. Minneapolis: Carolrhoda Books.
*Tobias is a 12-year-old boy who lives with his family in Greenland. Basic information about Greenland is given suitable for very young children. Easy-to-read and good for reading aloud to preschoolers. (There are other books in the series about Tobias.)*

Keller, Holly. **Geraldine's Blanket.** New York: Greenwillow Books.
*Gerald refuses to give up her bedraggled baby blanket. The text is short and the vocabulary is easy.*

Kennedy, Jimmy. **The Teddy Bear's Picnic.** La Jolla, CA: Green Tiger Press.
*The colors in the full-page illustrations of the children's song "If You Go Down to the Woods Today" create an enchanting mood. A record with two versions of the song accompanies the book.*

Mitchell, Joyce Slayton. **My Mommy Makes Money.** Boston: Little, Brown & Co.
*A short but descriptive book about 14 women at work. The jobs are varied and not stereotyped.*

Porte, Barbara Ann. **Harry's Dog.** Minneapolis: Carolrhoda Books.
*Harry's father is allergic to dogs and this is a BIG problem. This is a beginning-to-read book that enables the reader to find the solution by himself.*

Watanabe, Shigeo. **I Can Take A Walk.** New York: Philomel Books.
*The eight books in this series have Bear exerting his independence and taking a walk. Simple, large type and uncluttered illustrations make this book appealing to the young reader.*

Wheeler, Cindy. **The Complete Adventures of Marmalade.** New York: Alfred A. Knopf.
*Whimsical books about the adventures of a mischievous orange tabby.* **(Marmalade's Christmas Present, Marmalade's Nap, Marmalade's Picnic, Marmalade's Snowy Day, Marmalade's Leaf)**

# CREATIVE LEARNING

# CREATIVE LEARNING

The development of the young child's innate creative potential is largely dependent on early environmental influences. Ideally, the arts should be a natural part of everyday life. Music, stories and poetry, the spontaneous expression of feelings and emotions, the opportunity for creative movement, and experiences with color and a variety of art materials can be provided easily and routinely. Much too often, however, undue emphasis is placed on cognitive learning in areas such as reading and math readiness at the expense of affective activities related to creative development. This is partially due to the fact that growth in reading, language, math and science is more measurable and is therefore perceived as more valuable.

The child who asks "What makes the colors in the rainbow?" or exclaims "Look, the dewdrops on the windowsill look like diamonds with the sun shining on them!" is demonstrating a creative readiness to explore the wonderful world of color, design and movement and to identify with open-ended, artistic experiences. It is at this point that a sensitive teacher arranges space, materials and schedules to encourage each child to make the most of this magic time for growing and learning.

# THINGS TO DO WITH PAINT

- Trace hands or feet on a piece of brown wrapping paper (part of a paper sack is fine). Then, just for fun, paint faces. You'll be surprised at the creative creatures that emerge.

- Paint with a cotton swab. Dip the cotton swab into liquid tempera paint and make dot patterns on a piece of paper. Make dot trees, animals, houses, flowers, or whatever you choose. Use lots of colors! Remember to use a fresh cotton swab each time. Stick to dot patterns. Don't try to paint using strokes — a brush is better for that.

- Design with paints. Put three or four different colors of poster or liquid tempera paints in shallow containers. Use large sheets of paper and objects such as spools, plastic forks, cookie cutters, bottle tops, etc. to make designs.

● Paint with sand. Mix one cup of sifted, dry, clean sand and two tablespoons powdered tempera. Brush a sheet of paper with watered-down white glue to make a design or picture. Pour the sand mixture onto the glue design and then shake off the excess sand. (If you don't have sand you can always use salt!)

Plan your picture.

Brush design with glue.

Pour on sand mixture.

Shake off excess. Sand will stay where glue is.

● Use a drinking straw to "blow" a picture. Drop several different colors of liquid paint onto a clean piece of paper. Then, gently blow through the straw. Spread the paint by slowly moving the paper around as you blow to mix the colors. Keep the paper flat to dry. You will be surprised to see the interesting design of your finished product.

● Put finger paint all over a sheet of paper. Instead of using fingers, use a foam rubber hair roller, an old comb, or a potato masher to make designs.

# THINGS TO DO WITH CRAYONS AND MARKERS

- Say a word and select a crayon that "feels" like the word. For example: scary - black, sunny - yellow, winter - grey, Halloween - orange. Words to use might include stormy, happy, sad, frightened, beautiful, midnight, autumn, old, jolly, fun, shiny and dangerous.

- Decorate white Styrofoam cups, paper plates, and napkins with crayons or markers. (This is especially fun for a Valentine's Day, Halloween, or Christmas party.)

- Make a crayon resist! Choose paper and a crayon of the same color. Draw a picture being sure to crayon heavily. Paint over the crayoned picture with a coat of thin white paint.

- Turn hands into friends! Use a washable marker to draw eyes, a nose, and a mouth. These creative creatures can do all sorts of interesting things!

- Use crayons to decorate paper bags for lunches, storage containers, or fun costumes.

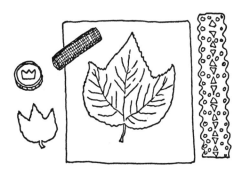

- Make crayon rubbings. Lay a leaf, coin, or other object with an interesting texture on a flat surface. Cover the object with paper and rub over it with the flat surface of a crayon.

- Decorate rocks with markers to make crazy creatures, animal friends, or special designs.

- Save big, thick catalogs to use for pads in art projects. Putting paper on top of a catalog gives a soft texture to pencil, paint, crayon or chalk projects. When the project is complete, tear off the top sheet of the catalog and throw it away so that there is a clean sheet for the next time.

- Decorate balloons for a special occasion or party. Fun party themes include circus animals, Mother Goose characters, and cartoon characters.

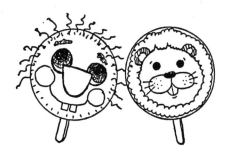

- Make a "mask-on-a-stick." First, draw a face on a paper plate. Then glue a ruler or stick to the back to make a handle.

- Scratch a picture. Use bright colors of crayons to color shirt cardboards or tagboard. Use a thick mixture of brown, black, or dark blue tempera paint to cover the entire surface. After the paint dries, use a paper clip, an old ball point pen, or a cuticle stick to "scratch" a picture.

- Color lace paper doilies to make fancy party table decorations. Use different colors to make the designs stand out.

- Use every crayon in the box to write the alphabet in living color.

- Draw pictures of make-believe animals that would make good pets. Tell funny stories about the pets.

- Draw a simple doodle on paper with a black marker. Turn the paper in every direction until you get an idea for a picture. Use crayons to make the doodle into a drawing.

Use 5 crayons to fill this jar with jellybeans.
Try to guess how many jellybeans you drew.
Then, count them to see if you were close.

Here are 3 circles.
Use your crayons to make each circle into something different.

Peter, Peter,
  pumpkin eater,
Had a wife, and
  couldn't keep her.
He put her in a
  pumpkin shell
And there he kept
  her very well.

Show what you would keep in a pumpkin shell.

# THINGS TO DO WITH
# PAPER, PASTE AND SCISSORS

- Make stencils using construction paper and scissors. Cut out a shape or design and place the stencil on another sheet of paper. Color or paint inside the stencil again and again!

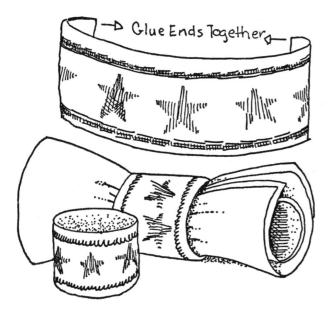

- Cut construction paper into short, wide strips. Glue the ends together to make napkin rings for everyday or special occasions. Decorate the napkin rings with crayons or markers.

- Fold a piece of paper into four equal sections. Draw a design on the top section so that it touches two sides excluding the fold side. Cut out the design without cutting the fold. Glue the design onto another color of paper.

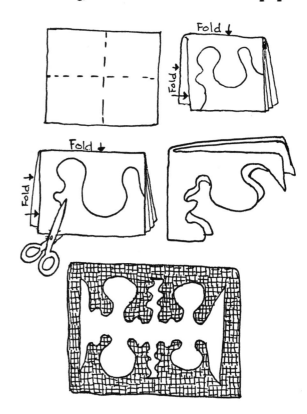

- Cut different shapes out of paper sacks and gift-wrap, etc. Arrange the paper scraps on construction paper to make designs or scenes for a set of very special place mats. For added fun, limit the paper to one or more colors, to shades of blue, to the seven rainbow colors, to holiday colors, etc.

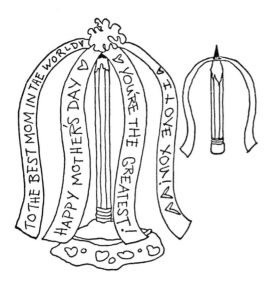

- Write holiday or special messages on strips of paper about six inches long. Push the paper streamers onto the point of a pencil and cover the top with a ball of tissue. Make a base using modeling clay.

- Glue a large magazine or calendar picture to a piece of heavy drawing paper or cardboard. Turn the paper over and draw puzzle pieces on the back. Cut the picture puzzle apart. Put the pieces in a box and see how long it takes to put them together again.

- Make interesting paper mosaics by arranging small pieces of colorful construction paper on the sticky side of Contact paper. No glue is necessary.

- Fold a sheet of paper to make a fan. Make a fold at one end. Turn the paper over and make another fold. Continue folding the entire paper and then spread the fan!

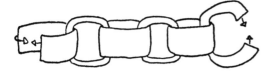

- Tear colorful construction paper into pieces of different sizes and shapes and paste the torn paper on cardboard or large construction paper to make a collage. No scissors allowed!

- Make a paper chain by cutting strips of paper and linking them together with glue. Make a bracelet, necklace, headband, or colorful border.

121

# GIFTS TO MAKE

- Gather small, unusual shapes of pasta to glue onto the top and sides of a small box. Let the glue dry. (Use a cotton swab to dab more glue around the pasta if necessary.) Sprinkle gold or silver glitter on the box for a shiny trinket box. Use shells or tiny pebbles instead of noodles to make a great reminder of a special field trip. Either of these special boxes will last longer if you brush on a thin coat of shellac.

- Make potpourri for Aunt Marie or any other nice person! Mix cinnamon sticks, cloves, and dried flower petals in a Mason jar and sprinkle the mixture with allspice. Let the potpourri stand for one week. Then, put a handful in a net bag and tie it with ribbon.

- String noodles on a piece of yarn to make necklaces or bracelets. To make colored necklaces, soak the noodles in water with a bit of food coloring and let them dry.

- Look through old catalogs to find pictures of things that family members would like for gifts. Cut out one thing for each person in the family. Give the "make-believe" gifts to the right persons and find out if you made good selections!

122

- Bake a cake from a store-bought cake mix. Lay a pretty lace doily over the top of the cake and sprinkle it with powdered sugar. Gently lift the doily. The cake will look just like it has been painted with snow by a magic fairy's wand!

- Choose a nice, firm orange to make a sweet-smelling ball to hang in the closet. Push cloves into the orange as close together as possible. Tie a pretty ribbon around the orange and make a loop at the top for hanging.

- Make a bookmark out of a piece of pretty ribbon or a sheet of brightly colored paper. Write a special message on it and give it to someone who loves to read.

- Decorate a plastic strawberry basket by weaving ribbon and yarn in and out of the basket. Fill the basket with seedpods or wildflowers to make an extra-special gift for a shut-in.

- A coupon book is a great gift for Father's Day, Mother's Day, Christmas, or other special occasions. Make "coupons" by cutting sheets of paper in half. Write or draw on each coupon a special service to be performed such as watering the plants, putting away clothes, helping wash dishes, etc. Staple the coupons together and make a construction paper cover.

- Make greeting cards! Homemade cards are so much more fun than the ones you buy. Cut out pretty designs from old greeting cards to paste on index cards, old boxes, or sheets of writing paper. You can also use pressed flowers, photographs, magazine pictures, fancy letters, and original drawings. Write or draw happy birthday messages or holiday greetings.

cut out hearts on an accordion fold, making sure not to cut apart the edges.

dried flowers on a lace paper doily are nice for Mother's day.

• Make extraordinary containers to turn otherwise ordinary gifts into something special. Try one of these or think of your own.

## DESK SET

Attach a doily to the top of a baby food jar with a rubber band.

Make a label & glue onto the jar. Fill with paper clips and/or rubber bands & give your desk set to someone special.

## PENCIL HOLDER

Cover juice can with construction paper. Tape in place.

Cut two circles from construction paper. Draw a lion's face on the small one & cut slits in the large one as shown.

Glue small circle to large circle

draw simple body on container

glue lion's face on container

Cut & curl a long paper strip for the tail

tape or glue tail to the bottom of container

## VASE

Tie a pretty ribbon around a bottle & fill it with dried flowers.

## SPECIAL PAPERS BOX

Cover a shoe box or stationery box with notebook paper. Decorate with crayons & give to parents to fill with their child's special school papers.

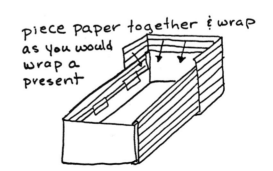

piece paper together & wrap as you would wrap a present

125

# MORE FUN THINGS TO DO

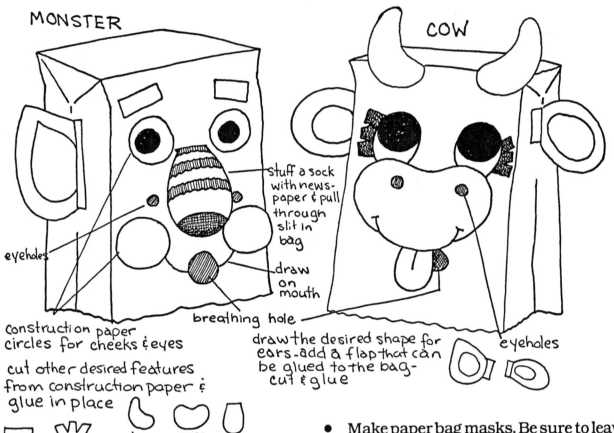

MONSTER

COW

stuff a sock with newspaper & pull through slit in bag

draw on mouth

eyeholes

Construction paper circles for cheeks & eyes

cut other desired features from construction paper & glue in place

eyebrow   eyelashes   horn   nose   tongue

breathing hole

draw the desired shape for ears - add a flap that can be glued to the bag - cut & glue

eyeholes

- Make paper bag masks. Be sure to leave big holes for breathing.

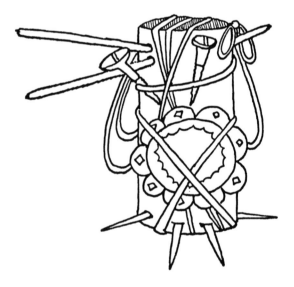

- Wash a window the old fashioned way. Use a cloth to spread glass wax all over the window. Be sure to allow the wax to dry. Then use a finger to draw anything you choose. Leave the picture to be admired for awhile and then wipe it away with a clean cloth. Shine and polish until the window is squeaky clean.

- Make a "junk sculpture." Collect screws, pipe cleaners, rubber bands, paper clips, pieces of string, old jewelry, toothpicks, and other odds and ends. Piece them together to make a one-of-a-kind creation.

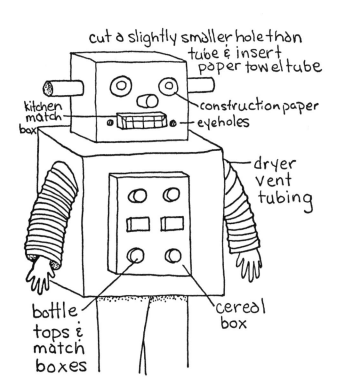

cut a slightly smaller hole than tube & insert paper towel tube

kitchen match box

construction paper eyeholes

dryer vent tubing

bottle tops & match boxes

cereal box

- Robots you are not, but no one will know if you make robot costumes! (Fun for Halloween.)

MONSTER MASH

- Bake a monster. Mold cookie dough into the shape of a monster and have a monster party!

- Make animal critters! Use squash, turnips, carrots, potatoes, celery, and toothpicks to create critters with personalities all their own. Whole cloves, cinnamon sticks, and paper clips can be used for eyes, ears, noses, and other special features.

- Celebrate spring by making see-through birds, bees, and butterflies for all of your windows. Pour small amounts of liquid glue into each cup of a muffin tin. Add a few drops of liquid food coloring and just enough water to thin the glue in each cup. Use watercolor brushes to paint birds, bees, butterflies, and other winged creatures on waxed paper. Allow the paintings to dry and then cut out the creatures and tape them to windows with transparent tape.

cock-a-doodledoooooo!

BROWN'S BARN

BAAAAAAA

MOOOOOOOO

- Find a great big box to make a house. Paint on windows and cut out a door. You can also choose to make an animal cage, a boat, a fire station, a fort, or a barn!

- Make and break a piñata! Stuff a paper bag with newspaper strips, wrapped candies and/or small toys. Tie the opening of the bag with yarn so that it is secure. Paint the bag with bright colors of tempera paint. After the paint dries, decorate the bag with designs cut from foil and gift-wrap or crayon and marker drawings. Tie the piñata to a long stick and take turns trying to break it as part of a special celebration!

- Pop popcorn and watch it popping! What makes it pop? Make popcorn critters. Provide glue, drinking straws, buttons and bows, pipe cleaners, paper clips, and twigs and watch imaginations soar.

paper clips

buttons

buttons

twig

straws

marshmallows

pipecleaners

straws

cloves

128

## PASTE

Make your own homemade paste and enjoy a cut-and-paste party.
You will need 1 cup water, ½ cup flour and a pinch of salt. Mix water and flour together slowly in saucepan. Add salt and bring to a boil over low heat. Stir until thick and glossy.

## SOAP BUBBLES

Blow soap bubbles. Mix 1 cup water, 2 teaspoons liquid detergent, ½ teaspoon sugar and 1 teaspoon glycerine. Use immediately.

## SAWDUST CLAY

Mold creatures and critters from sawdust clay.
Mix 1 cup of flour and 3 cups of water and heat to boiling. Remove from the burner and cool. Add 6 cups of sawdust. Slowly add water to make a mixture with the consistency of modeling clay. Store in an airtight shortening or coffee container.

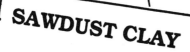

## PLAY DOUGH

*Make homemade play dough.*
Use these ingredients: 1 cup flour, ½ cup salt, 1 cup water, 1 tablespoon cooking oil and 2 teaspoons cream of tartar. Mix and heat ingredients unitl a ball forms. Add a touch of food coloring if desired.

## BAKER'S CLAY

*Create a dough picture.*
Mix ¾ cup flour, ¼ cup salt, water and tempera paint. Add water until mixture is as soft as cookie dough. Add a spoonful of tempera. Use fingers to shape the dough before sticking it on the paper.

## FINGER PAINT

*Finger paint with soap suds.*
Combine ½ cup dry detergent or a capful of liquid soap, and 2 tablespoons liquid starch. Beat with an egg beater until thick. Add food coloring to make different colored paints.

# PUPPETS!
# PUPPETS! PUPPETS!

Is it a sock, a sack, a bird, or a plane? Making and using puppets of all kinds helps children stretch their imaginations and develop creative self-awareness.

Creative puppets can be made from a wide variety of materials such as paper bags, socks, mittens, paper cups, construction paper, tongue depressors, and even hands or fingers. They can be as simple or as sophisticated as the children want to make them. They can be created to sing and dance, tell stories, act out parts in plays, demonstrate good health habits, and criticize or give good advice.

Playing with puppets will help children:
- enjoy vicarious experimentation in social situations
- develop speaking and listening skills
- build self-esteem
- provide interaction with peers
- overcome shyness, self-consciousness
- expose and deal with hidden fears and anxieties
- share personal thoughts and opinions in a non-threatening manner

More importantly, puppets are fun to make and use, and they encourage children to think and act spontaneously.

Glue ears to back of sack.

paper Sack →

BUFORD the BURRO

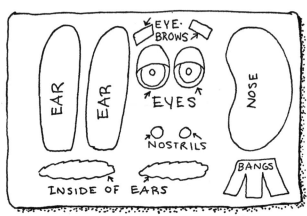

Make features from construction paper. You may use different colors of paper or color the features with markers.

Glue features to sack.

Draw a friend on your thumb.

Use washable markers to draw your puppets.

You can perform behind a table or desk, or even a cut-out sheet of paper.

Draw and cut out a figure from heavy paper. Cut two finger holes and you have a walking finger puppet.

finger holes

Here's another easy finger puppet. Use this pattern and draw any figure in the middle of any type of paper.

Cut off the fingers of an old glove.

Use a ball point pen or markers to make a fistful of puppet people.

tape

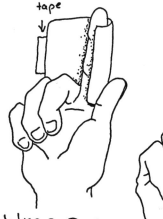

Make a whole handful if you like!

Wrap paper around finger and tape together.

133

Attach construction paper ears with glue.

Use markers to draw a face for a balloon bunny.

Draw and cut out a figure from heavy paper.

Tape or glue construction paper features to an empty cardboard tube.

Glue to a popsicle stick and you have a rod puppet.

Tape a stick to the inside and your puppet is complete.

Cut wings from construction paper and glue to back of bag.

glue halo in place

paper bag

TO MOMMY FROM JOY

Draw face and hair on white paper. Color, cut out and glue to bag.

cut halo from folded paper

Use crayons or markers to draw dress, arms, and legs.

An old fuzzy sock makes a friendly puppet puppy.

Curl fringed paper around a pencil for eyelashes.

My name is Lucky

Use an old dog collar, or make one out of paper.

Clue on felt or cloth for ears.

Make other features from felt or paper.

135

# Cut out, color, and paste the "fancy features" on a paper bag to make a puppet.

use eyelashes to indicate closed eyes or to place behind open eyes.

color grey  color pink

Draw a smile on your bag

Color and cut out the puppets.
Use the puppets to tell the story of Little Red Riding
  Hood, or make up your own story.

attach a popsicle
stick to the
back for a
rod puppet

# THINGS TO DO WITH MOVEMENT AND MUSIC

- Try to move two body parts to do two different things at the same time. (Draw on a piece of paper while tapping a foot, or wave an arm while winking an eye.) It's harder than it seems.

- Be a tightrope walker. Lay a jump rope in a straight line on the floor. Try to walk on the rope without letting either foot fall off the rope. Then try to walk a wavy line, a circle, and a figure eight.

- Sing to hear the sound of voices. Yodel, hum, and whistle, too. Learn the words and tunes to favorite songs and make up some new songs.

- Sing and act out the song "Here We Go 'Round the Mulberry Bush" by changing the words and actions to show some of the things you like to do.

"Here we go 'round the Mulberry Bush, The Mulberry Bush, the Mulberry Bush, Here we go 'round the Mulberry Bush, So early in the morning."

This is the way I ride my trike . . .
. . . walk to school
. . . read my book

yodel yodel lay hee hooooo

● Pretend to be the chief of a proud Indian tribe. Make up a dance for a special celebration.

● The human body can be used as a rhythm instrument. Try making rhythmic sounds by clapping, slapping your knees, or snapping. Stand and let feet slide, stomp and tap!

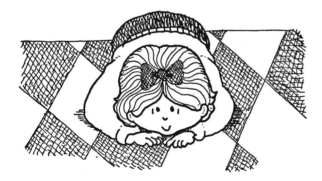

● Sit on the floor and try to curl up like a ball. Feel and act as round as possible and roll around just like a ball.

● Dance a scarf dance. Hold up a long, silk scarf. Now dip and twirl following the movements of the scarf as gracefully as possible.

● Listen to the record "Peter and the Wolf" (Leonard Bernstein and the New York Philharmonic, Columbia Records). Just listen the first time, then act out the story.

● Sing action songs and act them out. Good ones to begin with are:
"I'm a Little Teapot"
"Ten Little Indians"
"Where Is Thumbkin?"

● Finger paint to music. Move your fingers as you "feel" the music.
Try —
"The Surprise Symphony"
"The William Tell Overture"
"Swan Lake"

# Start with A and end with Z.
## Pretend to be each letter you see.

M N O P

Q R S T

U V W X

Y Z

# CREATIVE BODY TALK

Sometimes, actions speak louder than words.
Use your body to tell someone . . .

goodbye

move over

go away

come closer

Use your body to show . . .

. . . an elephant swinging its trunk

. . . a snake slithering along the ground

. . . a race car in an important race

. . . a buzzing bumblebee

. . . melting butter

. . . an egg beater

. . . a lawn mower

. . . a pancake on a plate

. . . a tree in a big windstorm

. . . a lazy, old crocodile

. . . a bouncing ball

**Creative movement**
© 1988 by Incentive Publications, Inc., Nashville, TN.

Use only your hands and arms to show how you would . . .

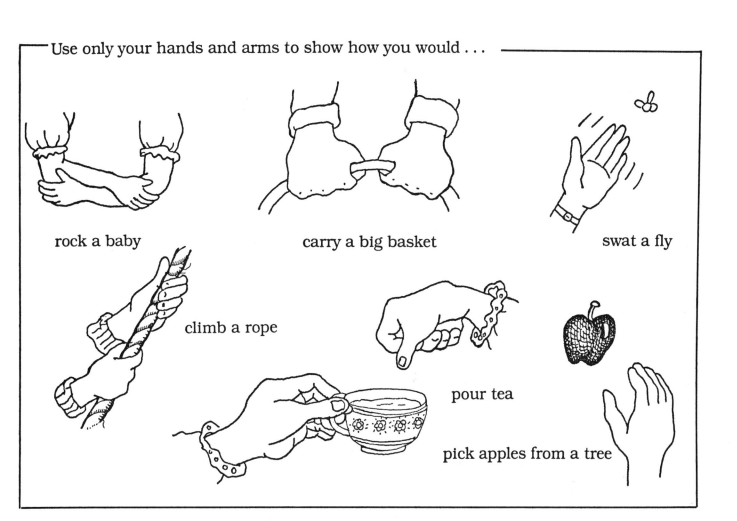

rock a baby

carry a big basket

swat a fly

climb a rope

pour tea

pick apples from a tree

Use only your eyes to show that you are . . .

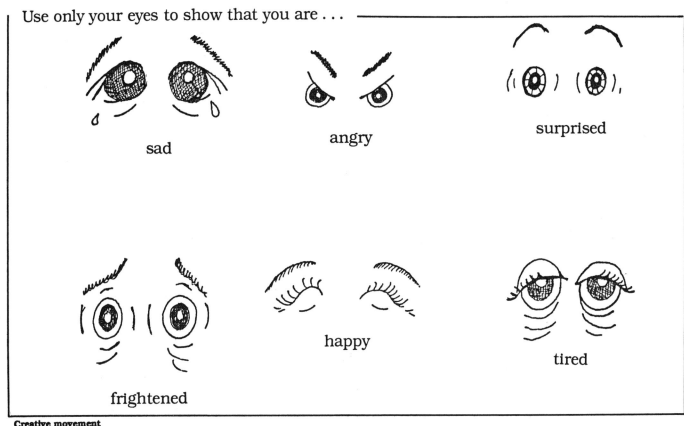

sad

angry

surprised

frightened

happy

tired

**Creative movement**
© 1988 by Incentive Publications, Inc., Nashville, TN.

# STRIKE UP THE BAND!

It's more fun with instruments that you make yourself.

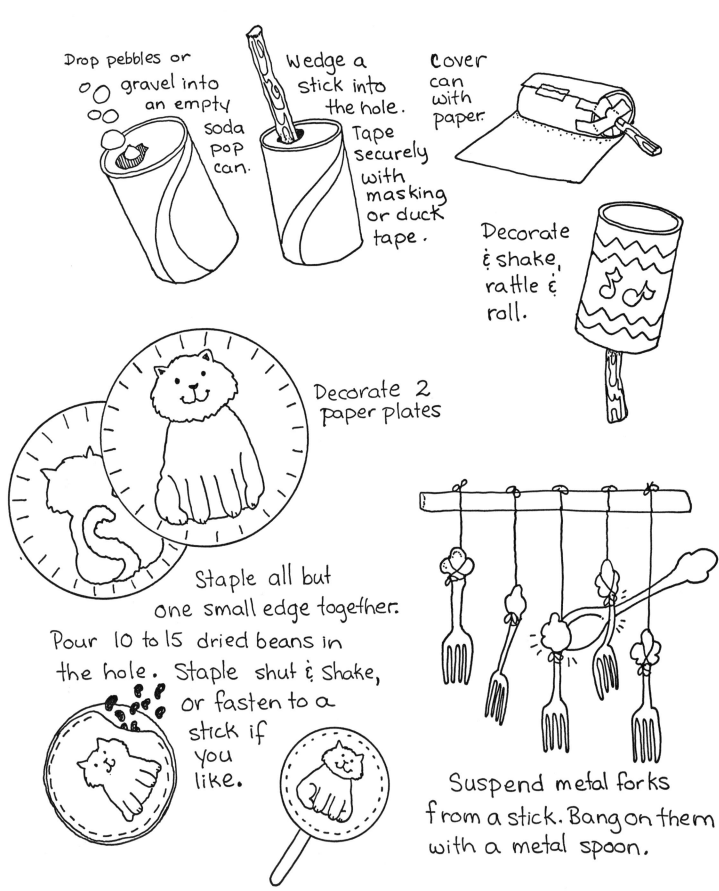

Drop pebbles or gravel into an empty soda pop can.

Wedge a stick into the hole. Tape securely with masking or duck tape.

Cover can with paper.

Decorate & shake, rattle & roll.

Decorate 2 paper plates

Staple all but one small edge together. Pour 10 to 15 dried beans in the hole. Staple shut & shake, or fasten to a stick if you like.

Suspend metal forks from a stick. Bang on them with a metal spoon.

## TOM-TOM

Punch a hole in each side of a large can that is open at one end.

Thread & knot ribbon through the holes— long enough to hang on a child's neck.

Tightly stretch a piece of rubber across the open end— securing with a heavy rubber band.

Inner tube works great— if unavailable try pieces of balloon or surgical gloves, or you can always use cloth.

## CHA·CHAS

Coarse sandpaper glued to wooden blocks makes a great cha-cha sound when rubbed together.

New pencils with cap erasers make great drumsticks.

## KAZOO

Use a pencil to poke a hole near the end of an empty cardboard tube.

Using a square of either wax paper or tin foil, cover the end closest to the hole & secure paper with a rubber band.

Hum into the end & you'll have a humdinger of a kazoo!

## CYMBALS

Flat pan lids are wonderful to use as a pair of cymbals.

145

## TAMBOURINE

①

Cut a 2ft. x 4 in. strip of heavy cardboard. Cut four circles out of the strip.

② Using a nail as a punch, poke a hole in the center of 12 bottle caps.

③ Cut 4 short pieces of string & thread 3 caps on each piece of string. or tie knots at the ends

④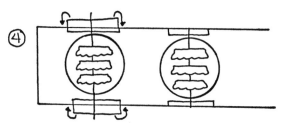

Tape a string of caps in each open circle.
Bring the ends of the cardboard strip together & staple. Tape over the staples with masking tape so no one will get hurt.
Now you have a fine tambourine!

## BASS

Remove one end of a very large can.

Pound a hole in the other end using a nail & a rock. (or a hammer)

Tape a broom to the side of the can.

Tie a knot in the end of a long piece of thick string or thin rope. Thread it through the hole & tie it tightly to the end of the broom. Make sure it's taut! Plunk away on your new bass!

INSTITUTION GREEN JEANS

## MARACAS

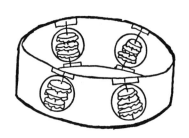

papîer maché over two light bulbs. Paint when dry, then bang the bulbs on the floor until the glass breaks, & shake shake, shake.

# THINGS TO DO WITH DRAMA AND LITERATURE

- Draw three faces. Make one face happy, one face sad, and one face angry. Make up a story about the three faces and tell why each face shows the feeling that it does.

- Find a picture in a magazine or a library book that shows people doing something (a family at the dinner table, a birthday party, people in a car, etc.). Make up a story to tell what will happen next.

- Save empty cereal boxes, coffee tins, etc., to set up a store. Put prices on the make-believe items and set up a classroom store for some creative buying and selling.

- Choose a hat for a day from a big box of hats. Select one you would like to wear to be somebody different. Put the hat on, try to think like that person, and then act out the role.

- Make these sounds and then act them out . . .
    . . . a zipper zipping
    . . . a motor roaring
    . . . rain falling on a rooftop
  Make up some more noises and ask someone else to act them out.

- Paint a silly-time tree on a big sheet of butcher paper. Tape the tree to a wall in the classroom to make a silly-time corner. When you feel really silly, go to the corner to tell silly stories, corny jokes, nonsense rhymes, and riddles.

- Get library cards! Visit the library as often as possible and check out books about things to know and do and most importantly of all, books that will be "just for fun."

• Paint a really big truck on a really big sheet of paper! Make up a story about the truck — where it will go, what it will carry, and who will be driving it.

• Pantomime is fun — it is acting out experiences without any words. Pantomime:

— unwrapping a lollipop, throwing the paper away, licking the lollipop, and then throwing away the stick.

— picking up a tiny baby, putting it in its crib, patting it on the back, and pulling up the blanket.

— taking a package from the mailman, opening it, taking the present out, looking at it, and then putting it back in the box.

• Think about what you want to be when you grow up — butcher, baker, police officer, teacher, doctor, lawyer, nurse or chief. Act out the part and have someone guess what your job is.

• Make up a funny story about a piggy bank that comes to life.

• Move several chairs together to make a bus or train. Select a driver, seat the passengers, and "hit the road."

• Read some favorite nursery rhymes. Tell how the people in the nursery rhymes might have looked, how they might have felt, and what they might have done. (How old was Little Boy Blue? Was he brave or timid? Did he blow the horn in time or did he get in trouble?)

• Use blocks, toy cars and trucks, plastic animals, and other toys to build a make-believe town. Give the town a name and make up a story about what goes on there.

- Pretend that you are in a hot air balloon floating over your house. Tell a story about who and what you can see when you look down.

- Play the "I see" game with three, four, or more people. The first person says, "I see something you don't see and it rhymes with groom." (Be sure the object is in plain view.) The person who guesses the right object gets to name an object next. Colors or beginning sounds may be used instead of rhyming words.

- Try to show different feelings just by walking. Walk happily, proudly, fearfully, and bravely. Add some walks of your own.

- Make up a TV commercial for a favorite food. Pretend to be on the air and present the commercial to the viewers.

- Pretend to be . . .

    . . . a spaceship blasting off
    . . . a goldfish in a fish bowl
    . . . an old truck on a country road
    . . . a kite in the sky on a windy day
    . . . Humpty Dumpty falling off the wall
    . . . a turtle sticking his head out of his shell

- Make up rhymes with rhyming words. It gets easier with practice. Here are some words to use.

| **and** | **bat** | **call** | **well** |
|---|---|---|---|
| band | cat | fall | bell |
| hand | fat | tall | tell |
| sand | hat | ball | sell |
| land | rat | wall | fell |

| **ring** | **me** | **fist** | **go** |
|---|---|---|---|
| king | be | list | no |
| sing | we | mist | so |

| **book** | **night** | **broom** | **day** |
|---|---|---|---|
| cook | fight | zoom | hay |
| took | light | loom | lay |
| hook | sight | doom | say |
| look | right | room | may |

| **bar** | **bed** | **ten** | **gold** |
|---|---|---|---|
| far | red | hen | cold |
| jar | led | men | sold |
| tar | fed | pen | told |

- "Read" and talk about one of these beautiful picture books.
  - **Gilberto and the Wind** by Marie Hall Ets
  - **Andy and the Lion** by James Daugherty
  - **Millions of Cats** by Wanda Gag

- Make up a story about:
  "The Little Witch Who Got Lost on Halloween"
  "The Easter Bunny Who Didn't Like To Hide Eggs"
  "Santa's Reindeer Who Hated Cold Weather"
  "The Heart That Fell Apart"
  "The Leprechaun Who Grew into a Giant"
  "The Dreidel That Couldn't Stop Spinning"

- Cover a card table with an old sheet or tablecloth to make a hide-away. It can become a cave, a desert island, a tunnel, or just a special thinking place.

- Make a collection of dress-up clothes — the fancier the better. Add lots of hats, shoes and jewelry (wigs are lots of fun, too).

- Pretend someone gave you a pet dinosaur for a birthday present. Tell what you would name it, what you would feed it, where it would sleep, and what you would tell the neighbors.

# MAKE YOUR OWN BOOK

**1.** Select a topic such as a seasonal theme or a unit related to animals, winter holidays, toys, community helpers, me and my family, safety, etc.

**2.** Cut four or five large sheets of paper in half for either an eight page or ten page book.

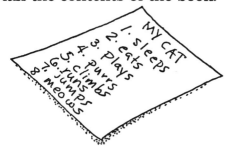

**3.** Plan the contents of the book.

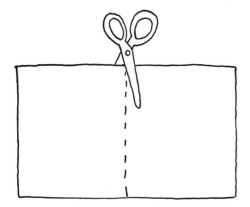

**4.** Work on one page at a time. Use crayons or paint to illustrate each page, or cut illustrations from old magazines and paste them on the page.

**5.** Arrange and number the pages.

**6.** Use construction paper or lightweight poster board to make a cover. Illustrate the cover any way you choose. (Be sure to add the author's name!)

**7.** Stack the pages of the book, place the cover on top, and punch four holes in the left edge of the stack with a hole punch. Tie the cover and pages together with a shoestring or a piece of sturdy yarn.

● This same process may be used as a group project to produce one giant book for the classroom reading center or school library.

Pretend this snowman just came to life.
Use crayons to give him a hat and cane, bright shiny
    eyes, and a scarf to keep his neck warm.
Then tell what will happen next.

# Tell the story these pictures show.
# Color the pictures.

**Sequencing/storytelling**
© 1988 by Incentive Publications, Inc., Nashville, TN.

Draw two chickens.
Make up a funny story about the chickens.

BARN THEATER
☆ TONIGHT ☆
HILDA & HORTENSE
☆ the ☆
HUMMING HENS

Poor Porky may be in real trouble this time.
Use your crayons to trace his trail and color the picture.
Then, tell his tale.

# BOOKS TO SPARK IMAGINATION
# AND ENCOURAGE CREATIVE GROWTH

- **An Arkful of Animals: Poems For The Very Young,** *selected by William Cole. Boston: Houghton Mifflin.*
  These delightful short poems featuring the animal world may be used as motivators for discussions about living things, for the simple humor of the poems, or just for brightening up a dull day. "What animal am I?" riddles or pantomimes would be logical follow-ups for the poems in this collection.

- **The Carrot Seed,** *by Ruth Krauss. New York: Harper & Row.*
  This is a read-aloud and act-out book about a dedicated young planter and the carrot plant he grows. Children never tire of "dancing" this delightful story.

- **The Color Kittens,** *by Margaret Wise Brown. Racine, Wisconsin: Golden Press.*
  This playful treatment of the mixing of colors is just the book to use to kick off a fun and fanciful exploration of the world of color. Hands-on experiments ranging from identifying and mixing primary colors to painting rainbows of many hues can be built into a science learning center. Plan a week of color days just for fun. On red day, red is worn by everyone, red things are placed on the science table, apples are served for a treat, etc. Round out the week with yellow, orange, green, and blue days.

- **Gobble, Growl, Grunt,** *by Peter Spier. New York: Doubleday.*
  This book which groups animals by their habitats portrays the animal sounds so graphically that children are sure to spend hours, if not days, cluck-clucking, gobble-gobbling, and moo-mooing to remind themselves of the wondrous sounds of the animal world.

- **I Know A Lady,** *by Charlotte Zolotow. New York: Greenwillow.*
  After hearing this story about a generous old woman and her way of showing love for two children who live near her, children will delight in drawing pictures to show things a neighbor has shared with them. A bulletin board labeled "Love Is Sharing" which displays the completed pictures can be a special reminder of the beautiful relationship of the old woman and the children.

- **Little Blue and Little Yellow,** *by Leo Lionni, New York: Obolensky.*
  This book goes beyond the simple story of a friendship between a blue spot and a yellow spot to present the concept of mixing the two colors to make one color. A logical extension of this exploration of color would be to mix yellow and blue food coloring to make green. Mix the green liquid with corn meal to make "gritty green goop." Use green crayons to draw designs of evergreen

156

trees or other green plants on light green paper. Brush paste or liquid glue thinned with water over the crayoned lines. Sprinkle the glue with the "gritty green goop." After the glue dries, shake off the excess "gritty green goop" and display the finished pictures on a bulletin board (with a green border, of course).

- **The Little House,** by *Virginia Lee Burton. Boston: Houghton Mifflin.*
  This little house steadfastly watches seasons come and go and observes many changes until it is finally moved to a new location where it can be happy. This same house provides a sensitive background for a group of mural or individual paintings based on the story's setting.

- **Over In The Meadow,** by *Olive A. Wadsworth. New York: Scholastic.*
  This is a delightful counting book to sing. In fact, it's so delightful that everyone will be singing it for days to come!

- **The Philharmonic Gets Dressed,** by *Karla Kuskin. New York: Harper & Row.*
  As children relate to the 105 people getting ready to go to work, they are sure to gain a better understanding of the backstage excitement that is experienced before a performance. A trip to a real concert would be a fine follow-up to this book. If this is not possible, listening to a good recording is the next best thing. Haydn's "Surprise Symphony," Mendelssohn's "Spring Song," or "Peter and the Wolf" are choices sure to hold young listeners spellbound.

- **Poems To Read To The Very Young,** *selected by Josette Frank. New York: Random House.*
  There's a good reason why this collection of poems has been around for such a long time and an even better reason why it has been reissued in a new, updated edition. Although this reason may not be evident to children as they enjoy the poems read to them, teachers will know that this book lives on as a treasure trove of springboards for creative word usage and language appreciation.

- **The Snowy Day,** by *Ezra Jack Keats. New York: Viking Press.*
  The simple words and beautiful illustrations in this book which portray a little boy's fun on a snowy day have to be shared and savored slowly. Torn paper snow people, snowy day pictures (painted on dark blue paper with white shoe polish and then sprinkled with silver glitter), or a felt board story about the snowman who came to life (with an ending supplied by the group) can serve to maximize the joy of this classic.

- **Stone Soup,** *retold and illustrated by Marcia Brown. New York: Scribner's.*
  On the day before you plan to read this book, ask each child to bring one vegetable to class. After reading the story, have the children combine their vegetables with your contribution of three clean stones, a handful of bullion cubes, a can of tomatoes, and lots of water. Simmer the soup all morning in a crock pot. The delicious aroma and wonderful taste of the soup as well as the joy of the shared experience will remain in the minds of the children for years.

# SCIENCE

# SCIENCE

Young children are true scientists by their very nature. Their unending questions, irrepressible curiosity, and zest for exploration equip them to absorb and process information at an amazing rate.

Taking time to question, wonder, explore, and ponder is basic to the creative nourishment of the scientific attitude in young children. As they discover each new scientific marvel, children should be encouraged to stay with an interest until their natural curiosity has been satisfied. As children are helped to arrive at satisfactory conclusions based on their own observations, the foundation for scientific thinking is being built. It is at this stage that their readiness for learning can be nourished and extended or discouraged and diminished. Often the adults responsible for organizing the child's daily activities will determine the direction that this innate curiosity and enthusiasm will take.

Providing opportunities to explore the wonders of nature firsthand; to experiment with "real" materials; to gain sensory images by feeling, seeing, touching, tasting, and smelling; and to verbalize these experiences will extend the use of this book. As children encounter more than one solution to problems and internalize the concepts gained from observation, experimentation, and classification, they will be well on the way to developing positive attitudes toward scientific exploration.

# THINGS TO DO TO HELP CHILDREN DEVELOP SCIENCE SKILLS AND CONCEPTS

- Place different items in a container of water (small pieces of wood, corks, screws, small rocks, spools, plastic picnic forks or spoons, coins, index cards, pencils, etc.). Allow the children to observe which items float and which sink.

- Have the children "go fishing" with fishing poles made of sticks and pieces of string. Help the children tie small magnets onto the ends of their "fishing lines." Place small metal objects such as paper clips and bobby pins in a fishbowl to be "fished out," or cut fish out of construction paper and glue the metal objects to the fish.

- Hit two stones together first above and then under water. Ask the children to tell how the sounds differ. Hit the stones together above the water several times, having the children cover their ears completely, partially, and finally not at all. Discuss the differences in the sounds. Hit the stones again, asking the children to listen to the sound with fingers pressed against their ears and then with hands cupped behind their ears. Discuss the differences in sound.

- Instruct pairs of children to trace around each other's bodies on large sheets of butcher paper. (Some assistance will be needed to see that arms are outstretched and that feet are not omitted.) Help the children draw facial features, hair, and clothing on their outlines. Have the children name as many body parts as they can. Discuss what various body parts do and ways to care for the body. Cut out the outlines and display them on a wall so that the children may match the "paper people" to the real people.

- Demonstrate how secondary colors are made from three primary colors. You will need freshly mixed tempera paint (red, yellow, and blue), four jars, a large chart, plastic spoons, and a paintbrush. Use tempera paints to paint a chart showing how each secondary color is made (see illustration). As you review the chart with the children, have them help make each secondary color. Ask two children to put four spoons of red tempera paint and four spoons of yellow tempera paint into the same jar. Ask another child to shake the jar to mix the colors and make orange. Continue this procedure to make green from yellow and blue, purple from red and blue, and brown from each of the primary colors.

- Demonstrate how a bottle filled with water and secured with a stopper or cap will sink whereas an empty bottle will float. Then fill the bottle halfway with water and have the children watch to see what happens. Finally, fill the bottle with the exact amount of water needed to make the bottle float just below the surface of the water.

- Make a "feely box" to motivate lively group discussion and to heighten children's sensory awareness and self-expression. Cut a hole large enough for a child's hand in the end of a shoe box. Place a collection of items of various textures in the box (sandpaper, scraps of velvet or satin, powder puff, eraser, chalk, crayon, paintbrush, small mirror, etc.). Ask one child at a time to reach into the box, pick up an item, and describe the item as fully as possible. This is also a good "tell and guess" game for free time. One child reaches into the box, removes an item and uses only five words to describe the item. A second child tries to guess what the item is.

## EXPERIMENT TO FIND OUT

- **Does air take up space?** Place a paper towel in the bottom of a glass. Turn the glass upside down. Holding the glass in a straight, vertical position, lower it under some water. Lift the glass and feel the paper towel. Lower the glass (with the towel inside) under the water again. Tilt the glass. Lift the glass and feel the paper towel. (When the glass is tilted, some air escapes and water goes into the glass.)

- **Is air real?** Blow air through a straw into some water. Blow up balloons. Boil some water and observe the bubbles. Blow on a pinwheel. Listen to air outside.

- **What does the word "evaporation" mean?** Put a small amount of water in a pan. Boil the water and discuss what happens to it. (It changes into a gas which cannot be seen.)

- **What objects will magnets attract?** Arrange several magnets of different sizes and shapes on a table with various other small objects. Example: nails, paper clips, pins, needles, pencils, crayons, coins, small boxes (like those raisins or hard candies come in), comb, etc. Experiment to find out which items the magnets will attract.

- **How are clouds formed?** Pour about two inches of hot water into a bottle and let it stand for a few minutes. Darken the room and place an ice cube over the mouth of the bottle. Hold the bottle in front of a lamp and observe the formation of the cloud within the bottle.

164

- **What causes wet things to dry?** Stretch a wet dishcloth flat on a table. Tie a second wet dishcloth in a knot. Which one dries faster? Why?

- **What causes things to ruin?** Cut a potato in half. Place one piece in a container of ice and one on the table. Which one turns brown first? Why?

- **What is a teaspoon, tablespoon, cup, pint and quart?** Measure to find out how many teaspoons are in a tablespoon, how many tablespoons are in a cup, how many cups are in a pint, and how many pints are in a quart.

- **How is butter made?** Put heavy whipping cream into a blender or a mixer. Beat and beat and beat. Soon there will be two things in the mixer. What are they? For a special treat, add salt to the yellow substance and spread it on crackers.

- **What causes ice to melt?** Place two ice cubes in an empty glass and two more in a glass with cold water. Which melts first? Why?

- **What things dissolve in water and what things do not?** Put some oil and water in a bottle. Shake it. What happens? Do you know why? Now empty the bottle, rinse it out, and put water and soap in it. Shake it. What happens? Why? Finally, empty the bottle, rinse it out and put some salt and water in the bottle. Shake it and see what happens.

- **Why do onions irritate the eyes and skin?** Peel an onion. What happens to your eyes? Why? Smell your hands. What happens to your hands? Why? Now, wash your hands with salt and water. What happens to your hands?

# PUTTING SCIENCE IN ITS PLACE

Set aside a nook, cranny, or corner of your classroom for a science exploration center. Then stand back to observe the learning that takes place as children engage in spontaneous explorations of the scientific marvels to be found there. Experiences with real materials that challenge the child to observe, question and experiment in order to find out "why" or "how" something happens are more developmentally meaningful than superimposed pencil and paper activities or highly structured, directed "lessons."

In planning the area, it is important to remember not to present too much at one time or to provide more stimuli than the young child can realistically handle. Clutter and confusion can be avoided by removing several objects before new ones are added and by discarding contributions once the interest level has diminished.

Nothing is more discouraging to a child's quest for scientific discovery than a science corner overburdened with dusty, cracked, or disfunctional artifacts and equipment vying for space with dusty rocks, birds' nests, and seedpods. The rule of thumb is clean up, clear out, and throw away in order to keep the science center challenging and exciting. Labeling objects and adding instructional charts, posters, and pictures adds to the learning potential of the center. Children should be encouraged to make contributions to the collection and should have ample opportunity for free time and directed exploration and discussion of their own and their classmates' contributions.

Basic materials to set up your "science place" might include:

- clock
- magnet
- magnifying glass
- hand mirror
- simple microscope
- hand lens

- measuring cups and spoons
- tape measure
- yardstick
- scale
- funnels
- scoops
- calendar

poster board sign can be hung from the ceiling →

**SCIENCE**

VOLCANO

hang a prism in a window

A terrarium is a wonderful addition

JANUARY

IS THERE A LOCH NESS MONSTER?

pertinent magazine clippings

big cushions ↑ can be stored under your table

a pegboard is useful when space is tight

SEA MAMMALS

REPTILES

a child's rocker helps create a friendly atmosphere

# MAKE AND STUDY COLLECTIONS

Ask children to contribute to specific collections for the science center. Add charts or a bulletin board display to present exploration questions and picture books to clarify and reinforce concepts being gained. Make sure that only one collection is presented at a time and that it is removed before interest wanes.

Objects can be observed, analyzed and classified by size, shape, color, sound, smell, feel and/or use.

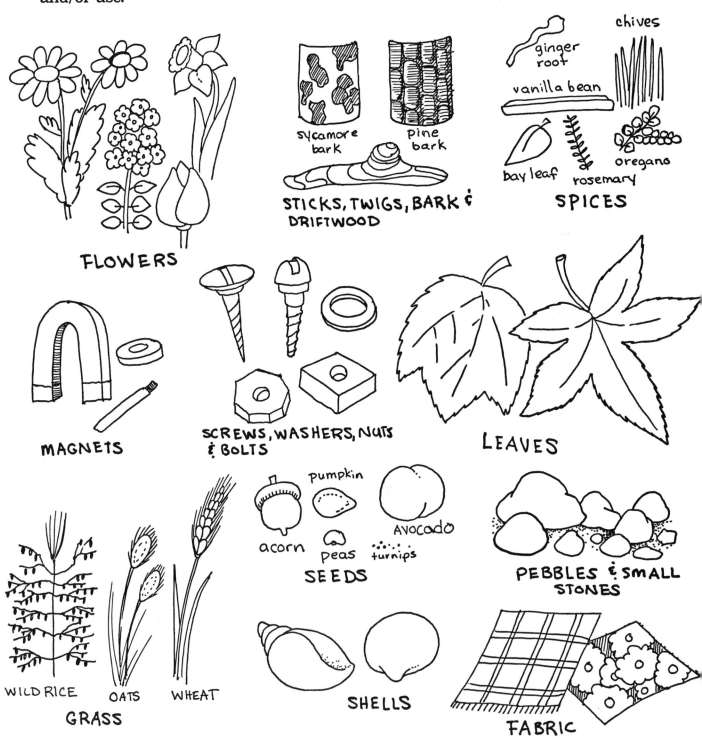

FLOWERS

STICKS, TWIGS, BARK & DRIFTWOOD

sycamore bark    pine bark

SPICES

ginger root    chives
vanilla bean
bay leaf    rosemary    oregano

MAGNETS

SCREWS, WASHERS, NUTS & BOLTS

LEAVES

WILD RICE    OATS    WHEAT

GRASS

SEEDS

acorn    pumpkin    peas    turnips    avocado

PEBBLES & SMALL STONES

SHELLS

FABRIC

# SCIENCE EXPLORATION CENTERS

Set up "free time exploration centers" by placing different objects, displays, collections, exploration challenges, and questions in the science center. Topics to be explored might include:

- rock collections
- shell collections
- magnets
- measuring

- color
- sound
- simple machines
- wheels

THE EAR

:ö: SOUNDS :ö:
- Is sound all around us?
- What part of the body catches sounds?
- What kind of sounds do you hear at school?
- How does sound travel?
- How do you make a scary sound?
- How do you make a soft sound?
- How do you make a loud sound?

wind chimes

a homemade megaphone allows a child to observe changes in his or her own voice.

Note: See instructions for making rhythm band instruments on pages 144-146.

# LEARNING TO COOK AND COOKING TO LEARN

Involving a child in the preparation of a simple recipe can become a marvelous hands-on science experience. As the child follows directions, uses measurement skills, and observes cause and effect and changes in matter, the awareness of these basic scientific processes is reinforced.

## COCO·LOCO·CAKE

1½ cups flour
1 cup sugar
1 teaspoon baking soda
½ teaspoon salt
3 tablespoons cocoa

6 tablespoons vegetable oil
1 tablespoon vinegar
1 teaspoon vanilla
1 cup cold water

Dump everything but the oil, vinegar, and water into an ungreased pan. Make three holes and put the oil in one, the vinegar in another and the vanilla in the last. Pour the water over the top. Stir with a fork. Bake for 30 minutes at 350°

## SHIVERY, QUIVERY GELATIN TREATS

1 package unflavored gelatin
1 package flavored gelatin

1½ cups cold water
½ cup boiling water

Mix unflavored gelatin with ½ cup cold water. Stir flavored gelatin in ½ cup boiling water. Remove from heat and stir in one cup cold water. Combine both gelatin mixtures. Pour into oiled, shallow pan or dish and chill until set. Let children use cookie cutters to cut out favorite shapes. Remove shapes with a spatula and enjoy! Makes 8 to 10 shapes. Increase ingredients to serve the entire class.

## CHUNKY PEANUT BUTTER BALLS

1 cup corn syrup

1 cup chunky peanut butter

6 cups rice cereal

Combine all ingredients and form "chunks" on wax paper. The more helping hands involved the better.

# GOOD-HEALTH MILKSHAKE

1 banana

1 egg

1 teaspoon vanilla

1 cup milk

2 tablespoons apple juice

handful of nuts

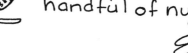

Mash the banana with a fork in a mixing bowl. Beat the egg and add it to the banana. Add the milk, juice, vanilla and nuts. Mix well until frothy. Pour into a tall glass and enjoy!

# ENGLISH MUFFIN PIZZAS

1 English muffin

2 tablespoons spaghetti or pizza sauce

grated cheese

toppings — hamburger, salami, olives, mushrooms, etc.

Brown the English muffin and add ingredients Pour on sauce Add layer of cheese Broil until bubbly

# EXPLORE THE OUTDOORS

- Be a rockhound. Find a shiny, round rock to use as a paperweight. Look for the most interesting rock you can find. Paint the rock. After the paint dries, glue small stones to the rock to make an animal or "critter."

- Plan an excursion to find evidence of living things. Before leaving, make a list of plants and animals to find. Examples: insects, flowers, weeds, birds, moss, lichen, etc. Try to name as many things as possible during the walk. After returning, use crayons and markers to draw what was observed on the walk. Arrange a bulletin board display for the pictures with the heading "See What Lives Here."

- Make a collection of as many different kinds of leaves as possible. Display the leaves in a science corner and discuss what kind of tree each leaf came from and where each leaf was found. Then use the leaves to make leaf people or animals. Glue a leaf on a sheet of paper and use crayons or markers to draw body parts, facial features, hair, and other distinguishing characteristics. This idea also may be used to make one-of-a-kind greeting cards, invitations, and booklet covers.

- Take a walk to find litter. After returning, discuss how the litter might have been left where it was found and what can be done to prevent littering. If possible, take a camera on the walk and snap pictures of the litter where it was found.

give your guest a stick to climb on & plenty of the leaves that you found him on

a wet paper towel will give your guest enough to drink

Cut out windows with a knife or scissors. Use masking tape to secure screen to the carton & cover sharp edges

- Make a caterpillar motel. Capture a visitor for the motel. Be sure to handle the critter gently, to feed it well, and to set it free before any harm may come to it. Read *The Very Hungry Caterpillar* by Eric Carle and enjoy the story of the transformation of the caterpillar into a butterfly as well as the fun illustrations of the caterpillar eating its way through the days of the week and through the book!

PICKLE RELISH

- Pick some interesting weeds and arrange them in a jar. Tie a ribbon around the top of the jar. Give the bouquet to someone who needs cheering up.

- Fly a kite on a windy day! Walk and run, prance and turn, and watch the kite soar, float, dance, and dive. Talk about how and why the wind keeps the kite afloat and discuss other effects of the wind.

- Take a large sheet of drawing paper and crayons or markers outside. After finding a place to sit, fold the paper in half. Without moving from your chosen spot for five minutes, look for three living things and three nonliving things. Draw the living things on one side of the paper and the nonliving things on the other side.

- Find a big rock in a grassy spot. Turn the rock over to find out what plants and animals live underneath it.

- Take a listening walk. Close your eyes and listen to all of the sounds. Talk about what you hear and try to determine the sources of the sounds.

174

Build birdhouses!
Use milk cartons, cottage cheese containers, or liquid
bleach bottles.
Hang the houses high and watch for the birds.

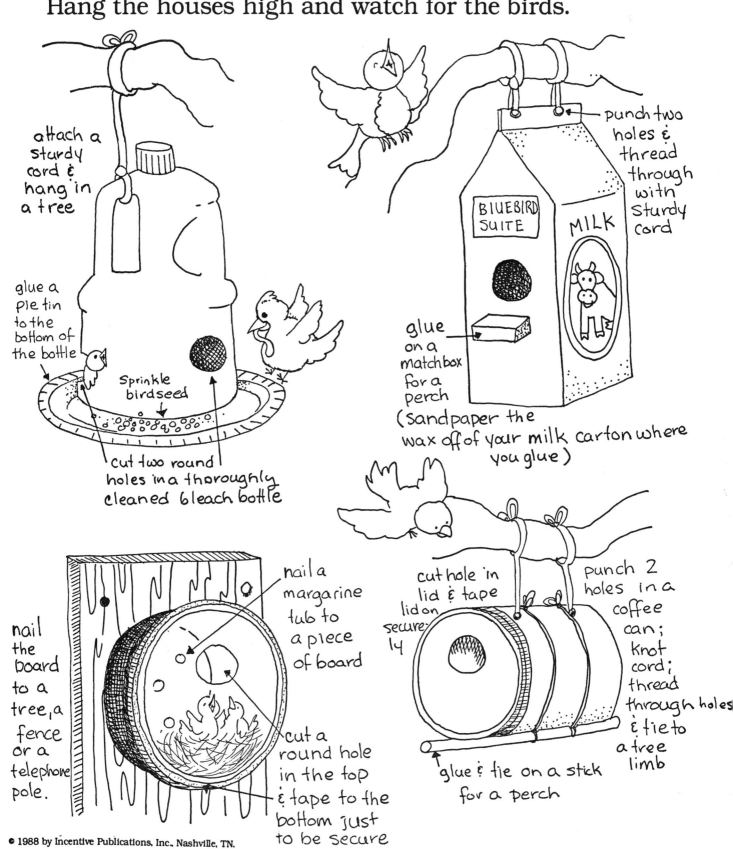

attach a sturdy cord & hang in a tree

glue a pie tin to the bottom of the bottle

Sprinkle birdseed

cut two round holes in a thoroughly cleaned bleach bottle

punch two holes & thread through with sturdy cord

BLUEBIRD SUITE

MILK

glue on a matchbox for a perch

(sandpaper the wax off of your milk carton where you glue)

nail the board to a tree, a fence or a telephone pole.

nail a margarine tub to a piece of board

cut a round hole in the top & tape to the bottom just to be secure

cut hole in lid & tape lid on securely

punch 2 holes in a coffee can; knot cord; thread through holes & tie to a tree limb

glue & tie on a stick for a perch

# THINGS TO DO TO HELP CHILDREN
# LEARN ABOUT PLANTS

- Have a seed study. Gather seeds from as many sources as possible (plants, trees, fruits, cupboard, etc.). Place all of the seeds on a table and study them. Compare and contrast the sizes, shapes, colors, and uses.

- Demonstrate how sun affects plant growth by planting some bean, cucumber, or squash seeds in two identical pots. Place one pot where it will receive direct sunlight and the other in a place where it will receive no sunlight. Water both pots at the same time with the same amount of water. Observe and compare the growth of the plants. At a later time, the same experiment can be conducted with both pots being placed in the sunlight, one being given the correct amount of water and the other being given none. This will demonstrate how moisture affects plant growth. (Conduct these experiments one after the other so as not to confuse the children.)

- Grow mini-gardens in eggshell halves. You will need an eggshell half for each child, soil, seeds, paint, and egg cartons. Help the children paint the eggshells, fill the shells with soil, plant a few seeds into the soil, and place the eggshells in the egg cartons. Set the egg cartons on a sunny windowsill if possible. Water them to keep the soil moist and watch the mini-gardens grow.

• Grow a garden from kitchen throwaways.

carrot top

sweet potato

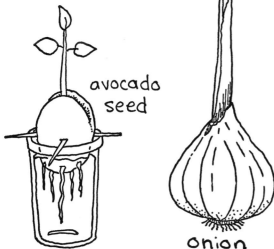

avocado seed

onion

• Ask the children to bring seeds to class in small plastic bags. Arrange the seeds on a bulletin board display to illustrate the categorization of seeds.

Things to talk about . . .

How are seeds carried from one place to another?

What seeds do squirrels eat?

Some flowers grow from seeds, some from bulbs, and some from cuttings. How do roses grow? How do tulips grow? How do potatoes grow?

• Adopt a tree. Select a tree to observe during the entire school year. Watch for seasonal changes, animal inhabitants, etc.

177

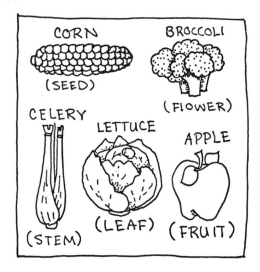

- Plant some seeds and watch them grow. Wet blotting paper and put bean seeds between a glass jar and the paper. Observe the seeds as they sprout. Record what happens in a daily journal.

- Discuss how different parts of plants may be eaten. Have the children look through magazines to find pictures of foods which are different parts of plants. Paste the pictures on a chart and label the part of the plant from which each comes.

- Find out what's inside a seed. Put corn or bean seeds into water to soak overnight. Gently open the seeds. Look inside each seed with a magnifying glass to see the tiny plant. Note the food the plant depends on until it can send out roots to get food from the soil.

- Find out how many birthdays a tree had before it was cut by finding a stump and counting the annual rings.

- Put a carrot, onion, potato, or turnip in a glass jar with some water. Watch and study the new roots as they begin to grow. How long does it take? What happens if the water evaporates? How can you keep the roots growing?

Color the flower red.
Color the stem green.
Color the roots brown.
Color the leaves any color you like.

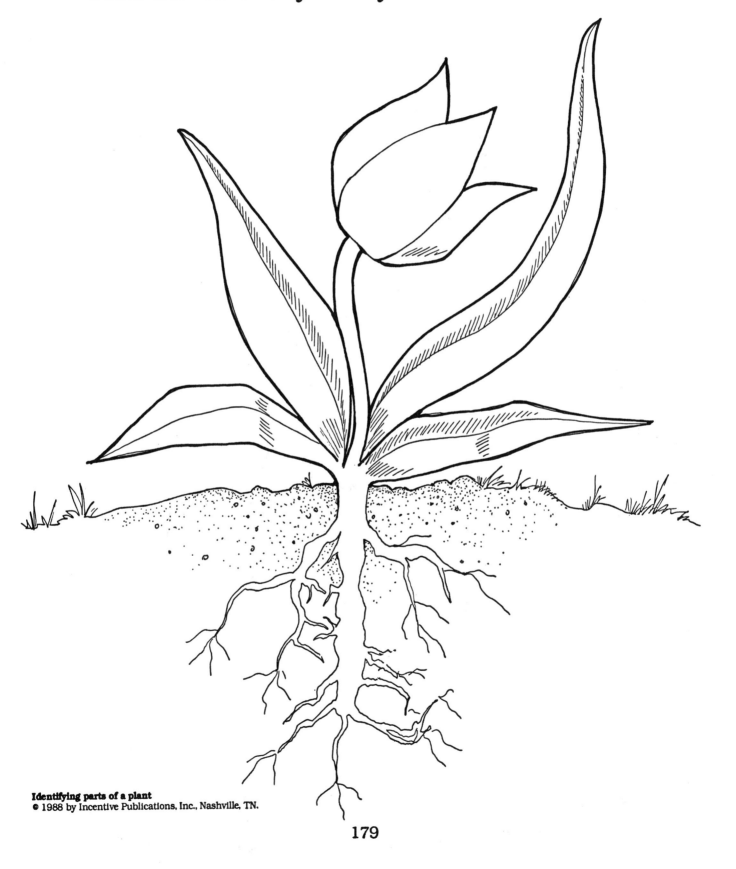

**Identifying parts of a plant**

ow does your garden grow?
Draw vegetables to show a special garden.
Color the plants and make up a story about the garden.

**Recognizing plants**
© 1988 by Incentive Publications, Inc., Nashville, TN.

All living things grow and change.
Find and circle 5 living things that will grow and change.

# Cut out and paste the pictures of the babies beside the correct mothers.

Color the 2 animals that are out of place.
Circle the 2 animals that are where they belong.

Draw a picture of an animal that would make a good pet for a boy or girl living in a big city.

Draw a picture of an animal that would make a good pet for a boy or girl living on a farm.

Draw a picture of an animal that would make a good pet for you.

# Color the animals that lay eggs and hatch their young.

# Plants and animals are living things.
# Find and circle 5 non-living things.

Plants and animals need one another to keep the balance
   of nature.
Color 3 plants.
Circle 3 animals.

**Differentiating between plants and animals**
© 1988 by Incentive Publications, Inc., Nashville, TN.

Human beings are living things.
Cut and paste the names of the body parts in the correct
   boxes.
Name five other parts of the body.

For a strong and healthy body, you need to eat food from each of the 4 main food groups each day.
Circle the food in each group that you ate yesterday.

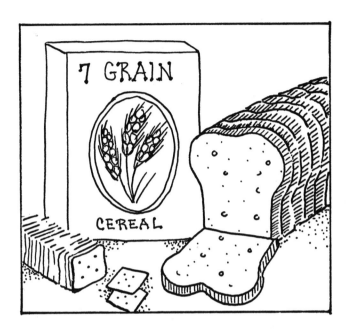

# Circle the foods that you like to eat.
# Color the ones that are good for you.

# THINGS TO DO TO HELP CHILDREN LEARN ABOUT THE SOUNDS AROUND US

- Reproduce the patterns on the next page for each child. Distribute and discuss:

  Where and when do we hear these sounds?

  What do they tell us?

  How is the message of the police officer's whistle or the crossing guard's whistle different from the physical education teacher's whistle? How is it different from your own whistle or a friend's whistle?

- Discuss frightening sounds:

  sounds in the night

  a loud thud in the house

  sounds I hear when I am alone

  a police car or fire truck siren

  the sound of a car wreck

- Discuss:

  What does the teacher use the bell for?

  What other sounds does the teacher use to send messages to the class?

  How does the sound of the teacher's voice change when different messages are being sent? Examples: "This class is too noisy. I want you to be quiet *now*." "I have such a marvelous class. Thank you for your good behavior today."

- Ask children if they can tell how someone feels by the sound of his or her voice. Use the following role-plays:

  ... a parent who has just found a messy kitchen where children have been making cookies without permission

  ... a child who has just found a favorite toy broken by a younger brother or sister

  ... a teacher on a rainy Friday when the class is especially un-cooperative

  ... a class when the teacher says, "We'll have an extra play period."

- Make several sounds. Let children take turns making sounds and guessing what the sounds are.

- Take a short walk around the school grounds. Listen for all of the sounds. Come back inside and discuss them.

- Select one item on the pattern page and list descriptive words that tell how the item sounds. Example: The bell can sound _____ (loud, sharp, tinkly, frightening, cheerful, happy).

191

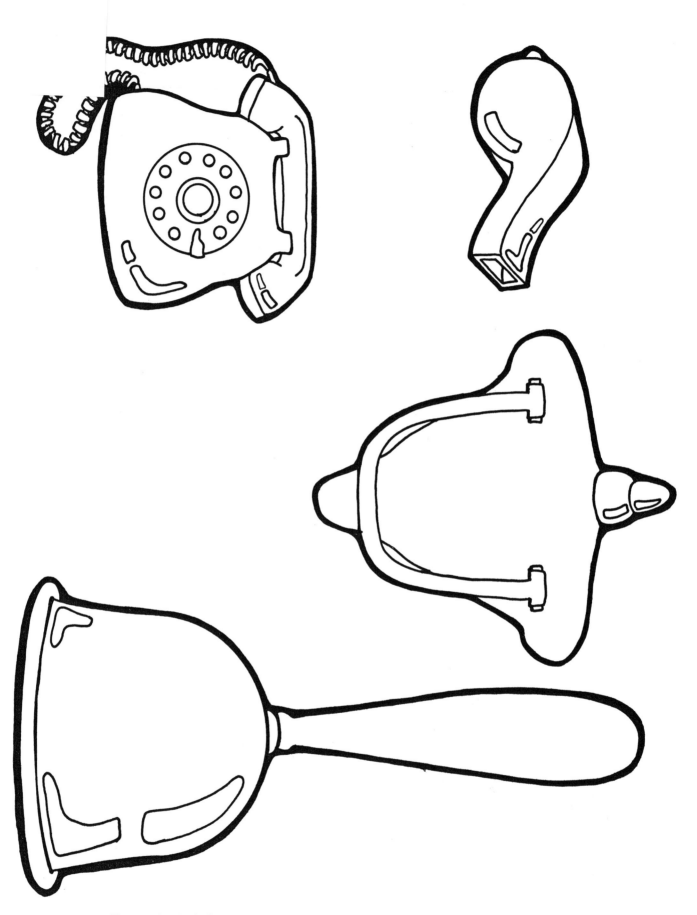

# Color the things that you can hear.
# Circle the ones that you would like to hear.

Color the things that you can smell.
Circle the things that you would not like to smell.

# WEATHER

Enlarge the calendar pattern on the next page to make a bulletin board display. Cut out enough of each symbol below to insure a monthly supply. Label envelopes for each symbol.

Arrange a time each morning for discussion of the weather. Have a child select and pin the appropriate symbol to the board.

**Things to talk about:**
- ☐ How does the weather affect plants?
- ☐ How does the weather affect animals?
- ☐ How and why do people who live in hot climates live differently from people who live in cold climates?
- ☐ What are some of the hottest and coldest places in the world? Can you find them on the globe?

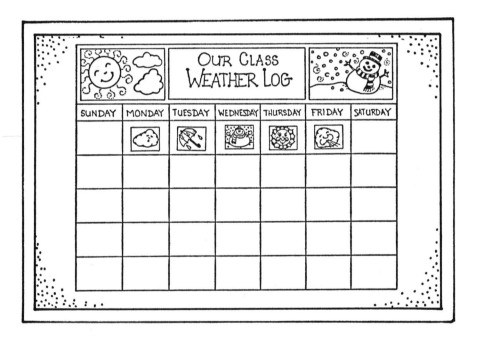

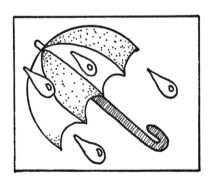

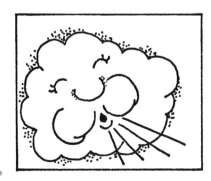

# OUR CLASS WEATHER LOG

| SUNDAY | MONDAY | TUESDAY | WEDNESDAY | THURSDAY | FRIDAY | SATURDAY |
|--------|--------|---------|-----------|----------|--------|----------|
|        |        |         |           |          |        |          |
|        |        |         |           |          |        |          |
|        |        |         |           |          |        |          |
|        |        |         |           |          |        |          |
|        |        |         |           |          |        |          |

Fill in month and dates and pin the appropriate symbol to the calendar each morning.

# THINGS TO DO TO HELP CHILDREN
# ENJOY AND APPRECIATE A RAINY DAY

- Find a good-sized mud puddle just after a rain. Use an old strainer or colander to dip all the way to the bottom of the puddle. Let the water drain through the strainer and see what you have left.

- When the sun comes out after a shower, go outside and make your own rainbow. Stand with your back to the sun and hold a garden hose so that the sunlight goes through the spray. Watch closely to see the rainbow colors.

- Collect enough "puddle findings" (pebbles, sticks, leaves, etc.) to paste on heavy paper for an interesting collage. Arrange the puddle findings to make an interesting design and paste them in place.

- Make mud pies and cakes (not to eat, of course) just for the fun of feeling, patting, and shaping. Mix the soil with water until it feels squishy and ready to shape.

- Make raindrop "splash" pictures. Drop "blobs" of different colors of dry tempera paint on construction paper. Place the paper outside in the rain just long enough for the rain to barely soak the paper. Bring the paper inside and help the child to tilt his or her paper from side to side, causing the wet paint to streak the paper and the colors to mix. Carefully place the finished projects on newspapers to dry. Talk about why the paint became liquid.

- Use Peter Spier's *Rain* (New York, Doubleday) as a springboard for a discussion about rain and its influences on people's actions. This is one of Spier's best picture books. He portrays two children's lively adventures as they find all sorts of unusual things to do on a rainy day. Later, place the book in the science center for children to browse through on their own. This is one book that children return to again and again, always finding a new reason to look forward to the next rainy day.

- Make up rainy day riddles. Examples:

  I am made up of lovely colors. You can sometimes see me in the sky just after the rain stops. I am a _____ .

  People hold me high on a rainy day to keep themselves dry. I am an _____ .

  Fold sheets of drawing or typing paper in the middle and cut them to make pages for a booklet. Print one riddle on each page and staple the pages together to make a rainy day riddle book for the reading table.

Make a paper airplane and take it outside on a windy day
   to watch it fly.
Try to figure out why the plane stays in the air.

Finish the snowy day picture.
Draw yourself in the picture doing something you
like to do.

Dressing to suit the weather is one way to keep your
  body healthy.
Circle the thing that is wrong in each picture.

Are you dressed correctly for the weather today?

**Dressing for the weather/health**
© 1988 by Incentive Publications, Inc., Nashville, TN.

# Tell what is happening in each picture.
## Color the pictures.

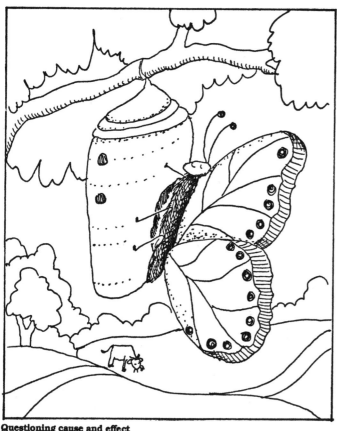

# BOOKS TO HELP CHILDREN DEVELOP SCIENCE AWARENESS AND CONCEPTS

Ets, Marie Hall. **Gilberto and the Wind.** New York: Viking Press.
*The wind becomes a thing of wonder and beauty as children relate to how it sounds, how it blows, and how it can be used.*

Fish, Helen Dean. **When the Root Children Wake Up.** New York: J.B. Lippincott.
*The beauty of spring is highlighted by a group of root children awakening to the birth of a new season.*

Forte, Imogene and MacKenzie, Joy. **Creative Science Experiences for Young Children.** Nashville: Incentive Publications.
*This resource contains easy-to-use units on living things, the human body, the earth and sky, air and water, magnets, and electricity.*

Heller, Ruth. **Animals Born Alive and Well.** New York: Putnam Publishing Group.
*The traits which make "born-alive" animals unique are made realistic through colorful illustrations.*

Hoban, Tana. **A Children's Zoo.** New York: Greenwillow.
*A photographic trip through the zoo embellished with a text of very few words allows children's imaginative language usage to flourish.*

McCloskey, Robert. **One Morning In Maine.** New York: Viking Press.
*This beautiful story of a family at the beach helps children to feel the mystery and the magic of sand, water, and fog.*

Provensen, Alice and Martin. **A Book of Seasons.** New York: Random House.
*A simple text and beautiful illustrations portray seasonal changes in a manner sure to capture and hold children's attention.*

Selsam, Millicent. **Greg's Microscope.** New York: Harper & Row.
*This simple and easy-to-understand treatment of the microscope and its use is perfect for young children.*

Spier, Peter. **Crash! Bang! Boom!** New York: Doubleday.
*Awareness of sounds and their origins is heightened as children learn about ordinary and extraordinary sounds made by people and things.*

Tresselt, Alvin. **Rain Drop Splash.** New York: Lothrop, Lee and Shepard.
*This charming, poetic text follows a raindrop on its journey from its first splash to the river that flows to the sea.*

Udry, Janice May. **A Tree Is Nice.** New York: Harper & Row.
*Bold and colorful illustrations are predominant in this book which focuses on trees and their uses.*

Zolotow, Charlotte. **Summer Is.** New York: Harper & Row.
*The delightful illustrations and poetic text in this book invite seasonal explorations.*

# MATH

# SIZES, SHAPES AND POSITIONS

Learning to recognize shapes and call them by name is fascinating to young children. Children enjoy mastering the words *rectangle, triangle, square,* and *circle* and using them in games and creative arts activities. Matching, copying and reproducing various shapes helps the child acquire important visual perceptual skills necessary for reading, writing and math readiness.

Noticing shapes in everyday situations also provides a good opportunity for developing concepts related to size and position. Children can learn to identify size differences and to use terms such as big-little/long-short/large-small/wide-narrow/fat-thin/and heavy-light by observing, matching and contrasting shapes. Shapes cut from paper, sponge or cardboard can be used to demonstrate positional terms such as above, under, over, on, before, after, between, top, bottom, first and last.

# THINGS TO DO TO HELP CHILDREN
# LEARN ABOUT SIZES, SHAPES AND POSITIONS

- Place three wooden blocks, three wooden cylinders and one wooden sphere in a bag. Ask the children to reach in and find: the round one; the one that is square; the one that is neither round nor square.

- Using a round container, a square container, and a collection of objects, have the children choose round objects for the round container and square ones for the square container.

- Ask each child to cut a picture from a magazine and paste it on cardboard or heavy paper. Then, have each child draw two or three large triangles on the back of the paper. Cut the papers into puzzles and have the children put them together again.

- Ask the children to cut shapes from magazines showing circles, rectangles, squares and triangles.

- Ask the children to find as many things in the room as they can that are squares, circles, triangles, and rectangles. Have them use their hands and arms to make each shape.

- Have the children sort buttons, beads, or any group of similar objects into appropriate piles by size, shape, or color.

- Mark the children's heights on butcher paper or something similar. Encourage the children to make comparisons as to their relative heights by asking who is taller, shorter, tallest, or shortest.

- Look around the room and select an object. Ask the children to find another object that is smaller or larger, taller or shorter, etc. Discuss the comparison.

- Take a rubber band and pull it as tight as possible. Mark its length on a piece of paper. Place a relaxed rubber band beside the mark. Have the children compare the two lengths. Stretch two rubber bands and compare these.

- Throw a ball three times. Mark the distances with a piece of tape. Compare the lengths. Have several children broad jump. Mark and compare the distances.

- Encourage the children to use directional words such as *in, on, under, behind, beside, next to, below, between,* and *above* by placing objects in various positions in relation to other objects. You might place a box *under* the table and ask, "Where is the box?" Encourage the children to use complete sentences.

- Draw a tree. Ask the child to draw a bird or plane *above* the branches, a nest *on* the branches, and toys or children *below* the tree.

- Ask each child to draw a circle at the *top* of a piece of paper, a square in the *middle* of the paper, and a triangle at the *bottom.* You may vary the shapes and their positions.

- Draw three circles. Ask the child to color the circle on the right red, the circle on the left blue, and the circle in the middle yellow.

# Trace the circle in the box.
# Color the largest circle blue.
# Color 5 circles green.

Can you find 5 circle shapes in the picture?
Color the circle shapes yellow.

Trace the square in the box.
Color the largest square blue.
Color 4 squares red.

**Recognizing squares**
© 1988 by Incentive Publications, Inc., Nashville, TN.

Trace the triangle in the box.
Color the smallest triangle green.
Color six triangles yellow.

Trace the rectangle in the box and color it red.
Color 3 rectangles blue.

**Recognizing rectangles**
© 1988 by Incentive Publications, Inc., Nashville, TN.

Color the rectangle shape red.
Color the triangle shape green.
Cut and paste the circle shapes in place.

Trace the dotted lines.
Draw a line from each object to the correct shape.

Color the large truck red.
Color the small truck green.

Circle the largest puppy in each group.
Make an X on the smallest puppy in each
  group.
Color 6 puppies.

**Using size words**
© 1988 by Incentive Publications, Inc., Nashville, TN.

# NUMERALS AND NUMBER WORDS

One need only listen to children repeating familiar nursery rhymes such as "Three Blind Mice" and "Ten Little Indians" to understand that a significant awareness of numbers begins at a very early age. Counting soon becomes an activity which brings the child great approval and reinforcement; yet, not every youngster who can reel off numbers actually comprehends their value or sequence — the child may have simply memorized a process.

The following activity pages are designed to provide meaningful experiences with numerals and number words. As you introduce these pages, you will find that some activities may be completed with little or no difficulty while others need to be explained, reinforced, or left for introduction at a later time.

Even for young children, variety is the spice of life. While repetition is important, you can help keep interest high by consistently using a math vocabulary geared to the child's ability level and by providing a good balance of "hands-on" projects (using blocks, measuring tools, money, etc.) and sequential pencil and paper activities (such as those provided in this book).

# THINGS TO DO TO HELP CHILDREN RECOGNIZE AND USE NUMERALS AND NUMBER WORDS

- Make number word flashcards from tagboard or index cards. Cut out corresponding cards with groups of objects drawn on them. Help the children use the cards to identify sets, count by sets, identify number words, and match numbers with groups of objects.

- Draw and cut out numbers from cardboard or Styrofoam meat trays. Make a game board by writing the same numerals on poster board with markers. Have children place the numeral cutouts on the correct numerals on the board. Use the numeral cutouts as game markers for other games.

- Provide the opportunity for children to group and count various objects in the classroom such as ten crayons, six books, five pencils, etc. Make a game out of this activity by appointing one child "caller." The caller asks another child to bring him or her a specific number of an object. Example: "Sally, bring me eight blocks." If the child "called" is successful, he or she becomes the caller.

- Make color-by-numeral or color-by-number word puzzles on shirt cardboards or box tops. Have the children work together to complete the puzzles.

- Help children look through old magazines for numbers to cut out and paste on sheets of construction paper in sequence (1 to 10, 1 to 20, etc.) or in collage fashion. Display the finished products in the room for "conversation pieces."

- Use index cards and markers to make a set of number word/numeral puzzle cards. Have children fit the cards together.

- Make up number stories about the numbers 1-10 and read nursery rhymes containing these numbers. Each time a number is read the children should hold up fingers to show that number. Example: one, two, buckle my shoe.

# FINGER PLAYS, GAMES, NURSERY RHYMES AND SONGS

The use of simple finger plays, nursery rhymes and songs as a regular fun part of the day will help develop and strengthen number concepts and skills. Try this old favorite for starters.

## THIS OLD MAN

This old man, he played one,
*hold up one finger*

He played knick-knack on his thumb.
*tap your thumbs together*

Knick-knack, paddy-whack,
give the dog a bone,
*clap your hands on your knees;*
*clap your hands together;*
*then hold out one hand as if you*
*were giving a bone to a dog*

This old man came rolling home.
*make a rolling motion with your hands*

This old man, he played two,
*hold up two fingers*

He played knick-knack on his shoe.
*touch your shoe, repeat lines 3 and 4*

This old man, he played three,
*hold up three fingers*

He played knick-knack on his knee.
*touch your knee, repeat lines 3 and 4*

This old man, he played four,
*hold up four fingers*

He played knick-knack on the floor.
*touch the floor, repeat lines 3 and 4*

This old man, he played five,
*hold up five fingers*

He played knick-knack on his drive.
*touch the floor, repeat lines 3 and 4*

This old man, he played six,
*hold up six fingers*

He played knick-knack on his sticks.
*Tap your pointing fingers together,*
*repeat lines 3 and 4*

This old man, he played seven,
*hold up seven fingers*

He played knick-knack along to Devon.
*point away from you, repeat lines 3 and 4*

This old man, he played eight,
*hold up eight fingers*

He played knick-knack on his pate.
*touch your head, repeat lines 3 and 4*

This old man, he played nine,
*hold up nine fingers*

He played knick-knack on his spine.
*touch your back, repeat lines 3 and 4*

This old man, he played ten,
*hold up ten fingers*

He played knick-knack now and then.
*clap your hands, repeat lines 3 and 4*

Other rhymes you might use
are *One, Two, Buckle My Shoe*
and *Two Birds On A Stone.*

# How many boys are here?
# Write the numeral.

# One kite is flying high.
## Write the number word.

one

**Recognizing and writing number words**
© 1988 by Incentive Publications, Inc., Nashville, TN.

# How many girls are playing?
# Write the numeral.

2

Count the dolls.
Write the number word.
Use 2 crayons to color the dolls.

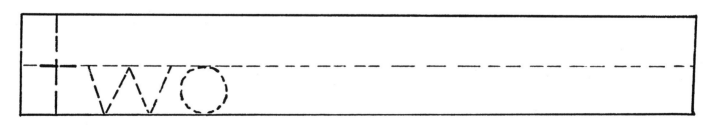

# How many rabbits are eating?
## Write the numeral.

Count the carrots.
Write the number word.
Color the carrots orange.

How many children are having birthdays?
Write the numeral.

**Recognizing and writing numerals**
© 1988 by Incentive Publications, Inc., Nashville, TN.

Count the presents.
Write the number word.
Color the present you would like to have.

four

# How many birds are flying?
# Write the numeral.

Count the birdhouses.
Write the number word.
Use different crayons to color the houses.

f i v e

**Recognizing and writing number words**
© 1988 by Incentive Publications, Inc., Nashville, TN.

# How many mother hens are here?
## Write the numeral.

Count the baby chicks.
Write the number word.
Color the chicks.

S I X

**Recognizing and writing number words**
© 1988 by Incentive Publications, Inc., Nashville, TN.

# How many painters are painting?
# Write the numeral.

**Recognizing and writing numerals**
© 1988 by Incentive Publications, Inc., Nashville, TN.

Count the paint buckets.
Write the number word.
Draw a paintbrush for each bucket.
Count the brushes.

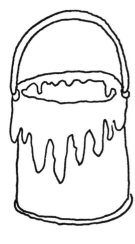

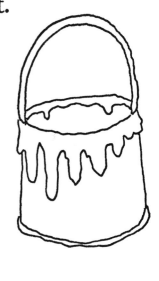

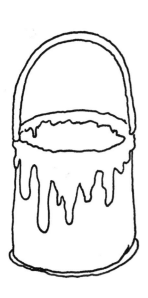
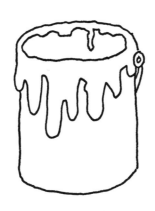
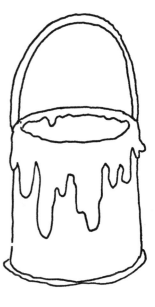

seven

How many clowns are here?
Write the numeral.

Count the hats.
Write the number word.
Color the hats red and yellow.

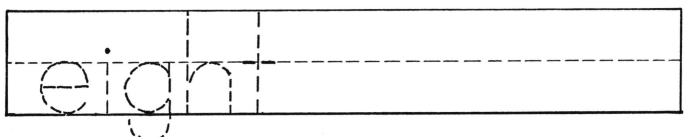

# How many cookies are here?
# Write the numeral.

# Count the glasses of milk.
# Write the number word.

nine

**Recognizing and writing number words**
© 1988 by Incentive Publications, Inc., Nashville, TN.

# How many monkeys are in the trees?
## Write the numeral.

How many bananas do you see?
Write the number word.
Color the bananas yellow.

ten

**Recognizing and writing number words**
© 1988 by Incentive Publications. Inc.. Nashville. TN.

# Cut and paste the numerals in the correct boxes.

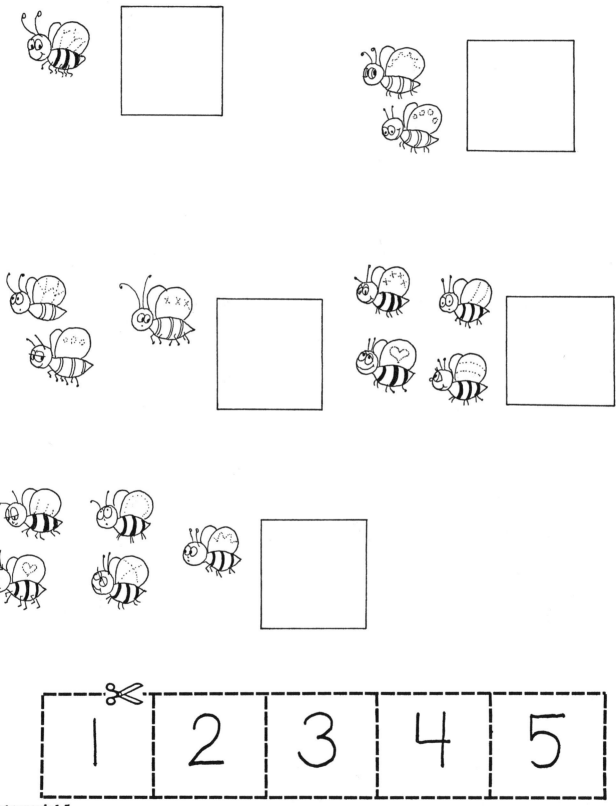

# Cut and paste the numerals in the correct boxes.

Count the candies.
Write the correct numeral in each box.

how many? _____

how many? _____

how many? _____

# SETS

Simply explained, sets are objects which are grouped together. The objects may be the same or different. As children play, they are unknowingly putting sets together. It is important to realize that until children are able to manipulate sets in a directed manner, a full understanding will probably not be gained. Activities should relate not only to what children know, but to the way they integrate this understanding into real-life situations. Important concepts such as first, second or third; first and last; greater than and less than; equal to; and one-to-one matching are developed as children work with sets.

Encourage the children to play with various objects such as blocks, crayons, toys, etc. Have the children sort objects into sets by putting toys with wheels into one box and toys without wheels into another box. Then, have the children count each set (items in each box) and discuss which is greater or lesser; how many are red, blue, etc. The children are not only beginning to understand the concept of sets, but they are also classifying by a common attribute: color, shape, greater, lesser, etc.

# THINGS TO DO TO HELP CHILDREN LEARN ABOUT SETS

- Use a large, colored plastic egg as a container for this activity (the kind hosiery comes in). Cut out 12 cardboard eggs to fit inside the plastic egg. On seven cards, draw one to six chicks; on the remaining cards, draw corresponding numbers of eggs. Give one set to the child and keep the other set. Select a card, hold it up, and ask the child to hold up the card from his or her set that: shows the same number; shows one more; shows one less. Continue until all the cards have been used.

- Arrange sets of familiar objects on the table such as spoons, books, blocks, pencils, and cups (each containing one to five members). Ask the child to find two sets that are alike, the set of books and the set of blocks, the set that matches the pencils, and the set that is greater than the cups.

- Put out two more chairs than the number of children and ask: "Do we have enough children for chairs? Do we have enough chairs? How many chairs are here? How many children are here? How many more children do we need to have the same number of children and chairs?"

- For this activity you will need three plastic forks and four plastic knives. Ask the child to pair the forks and knives and then tell which set has fewer.

- Have the children match sets of dots using dominoes. Selecting dominoes whose dots add up to a specific number is a good activity for the child who has developed the concept of number value.

- Match hard candy, mints, raisins, pieces of cookies or popped popcorn to numerals on cards. If a child is correct, he or she gets to eat the set!

- Draw five rows of five circles. On the first row, draw a "smiley face" in one circle. Add one more smiley face to each row, ending with five faces on the fifth row. Use these to talk about one more, one less, one-to-one, first, second, third, and first and last.

- Have each child take a handful of dry cereal or beans in each hand and then place each set on the table separately. Ask: "Do these sets have the same number? Does one set have more? How can you tell? How can you find out?"

- Place four mittens (two pairs) in a bag (each pair being different). Ask the child, "How many mittens must you take out before you have a matching pair?" Then, have the child try it!

- Make number cards from one to four. Place the cards in a paper bag. Mark a starting and finishing line on the carpet or floor with a piece of tape. Have the children stand on the starting line and pass the sack from child to child, each drawing one card. The child then takes the number of steps indicated on the card. The first player to make it to the finish line is the winner.

- See what children can build using clay and ten toothpicks. Vary the number of toothpicks and continue the activity for as long as the children are interested.

# How many are in each set?
## Write the numeral.

Counting by sets
© 1988 by Incentive Publications, Inc., Nashville, TN.

# TIME AND MEASUREMENT

"Look how tall I am!" "Only two more days until my birthday." "What time do we have lunch?" As young children talk, questions and comments such as these are heard over and over again. Children view time and space factors in relation to their own personal interests and concerns.

In developing readiness for beginning concepts related to time and measurement, it is important to relate planned learning experiences to everyday events. Calling attention to the clock and calendar as important tools for organizing our days, showing that thermometers and scales give useful information, and demonstrating how measuring cups and spoons are used provide children with a better understanding of the use of time and measurement.

Young children are conscious of "parts of things" in their environment and are very interested in dividing things into two or more parts if there is something to be shared. It is not at all uncommon, however, to hear a child say "I want the bigger half" when a treat is being divided into two parts.

You can help children use terms such as two parts, one-half, both, divide, and double as they relate to familiar objects.

The child may be ready to measure one-half cup of honey and one cup of milk for a recipe, recognizing the difference and noting that it takes two half-cups to make one full cup. The child may also observe that one shoe is one-half of one pair and that it takes two socks to make a pair of socks. Experiences of this nature are developmentally healthy and should be continued to the full extent of the child's readiness to learn.

Provide stimulation and guidance and let each child grow at his or her own rate. It may take a little longer, but the child's positive feeling for math will make it worth the wait.

# THINGS TO DO TO HELP CHILDREN
# LEARN ABOUT TIME AND MEASUREMENT

- Help each child make a paper chain with as many loops as there are days left until his or her next birthday, until Christmas, until summer vacation, or until some other special time. Then, make a ritual of breaking and removing one loop each day and counting the number of loops to see how many days are left to wait.

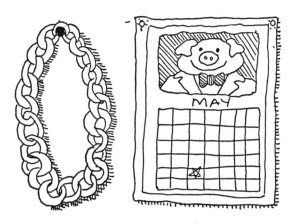

- For extra fun, use the nursery rhyme "Hickory Dickory Dock" as a counting rhyme.

  Hickory Dickory Dock,
  The mouse ran up the clock;
  The clock struck one,
  The mouse ran down,
  Hickory Dickory Dock

- Provide a paper plate, construction paper hands, and a brad for each child to make a clock face. Ask each child to move the hands to show bedtime, lunchtime, etc.

Change the time (the clock struck three) and ask the children to point to that numeral on the clock.

250

- Buy a large calendar with a separate page for each month of the year. Help the children mark special dates with pictures or stickers. Birthdays, holidays, parties, vacations and the first day of school make very important dates to anticipate. The number of days of perfect attendance at school or number of days without forgetting a certain task will serve to highlight the importance of the calendar in everyday life.

- Ask the children to locate and count all of the clocks and watches in the classroom. Then provide magazines and catalogs and help the children look for and cut out pictures of different kinds of timepieces. Try to find a clock radio, pocket and wrist watches, digital clocks and watches, grandfather clocks, etc.

- Use calendars to help children keep personal records of important events for one month. Provide the necessary help to fill in the month and numerals. Set aside a daily time to discuss the weather and assist the children in drawing sunny faces for the days with no rain, etc.

- Display two different containers and ask which will hold the most. Demonstrate the answer by filling one container with water, rice, peas, sand, seeds or popcorn. Attempt to pour that ingredient from one container into the other. Which contains the most and which contains the least?

- Compare a pint and a quart. Compare a liter bottle and a ten-ounce bottle. Compare a pint, quart and gallon. Experiment with how many pints are in a quart, how many quarts in a gallon, etc.

- Experiment with containers of different shapes that hold varying amounts. Count the number of jars, cups or glasses it takes to fill various containers.

- Measure popcorn before it is popped. Have the children choose a container to hold the popped corn. After popping, ask if the container was large enough and if it could hold more popcorn.

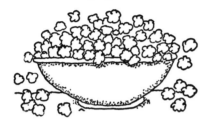

- Use a set of graduated plastic measuring cups to help the children discover that two half-cups are equal to one cup.

- Give each child three socks (a pair and one odd sock), and three shoes (also a pair and one odd one). Have each child match the pair of socks and the pair of shoes.

- Use two oranges, apples or cupcakes. Cut one into equal parts and the other into unequal parts. Have the child pick or match the equal parts. Stress the concept of equivalent parts and one-half when talking to the child.

- Let one child cut cupcakes, pancakes, soft cookies, pieces of fudge, or brownies into two equal parts. Another child then gets first choice. Talk about equal parts and one-half during the activity.

- Trace circles on colored construction paper and cut them out. Have the children fold several circles in half and cut them into equal parts. Have each child paste one half of a circle onto a piece of paper. Label it one-half. The children may use the remaining halves to make designs on other pieces of paper.

# Which one would you use to measure:

- ½ cup of milk?
- 1 teaspoon of sugar?
- your body temperature?
- your weight?

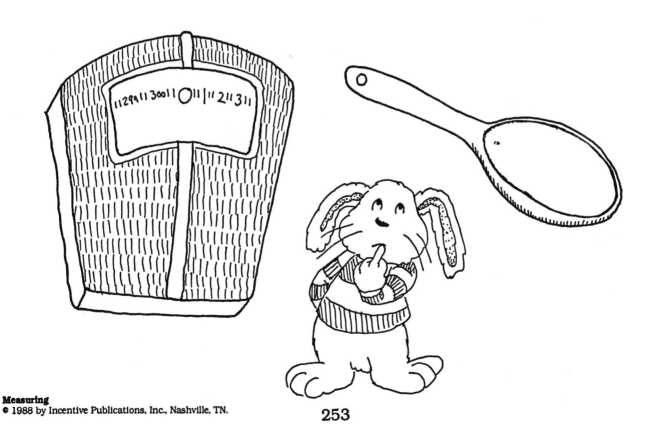

This is a whole cake.

Trace the line to cut the
the cake in half.

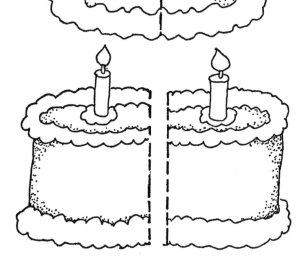

Each part of the cake
is one-half.

This is the way we write one-half.

Write ½ on each half of the cake.

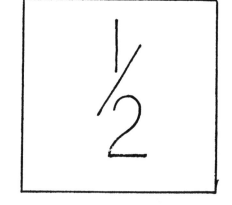

**Finding parts of things (concept of ½)**
© 1988 by Incentive Publications, Inc., Nashville, TN.

The short hand tells the hour.
The long hand tells the minutes.
This clock shows four o'clock.
Trace all the numerals.
Trace the short hand that tells the hour.

# What time does each clock show?

_____ o'clock

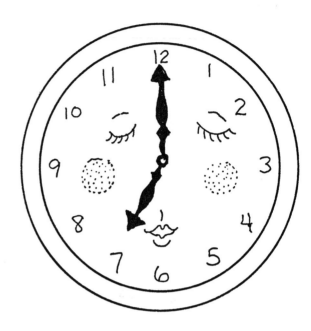

_____ o'clock

_____ o'clock

_____ o'clock

**Telling time**
© 1988 by Incentive Publications, Inc., Nashville, TN.

# BOOKS TO DEVELOP MATH READINESS

Adler, Irvin and Ruth. **Sets and Numbers for the Very Young.** New York: John Day Co.
- *a wealth of creative ways to introduce the concepts of sets, numbers, shapes, left/right, etc. (Resource book for child and parent/teacher to share.)*

Allington, Richard L. **Beginning To Learn About Numbers.** Milwaukee: Raintree Childrens Books.
- *the numerals 1-10 are introduced through a counting game, with the correct number being determined by clues in the lovely color illustrations.*

Anno, Mitsumasa. **Anno's Counting Book.** New York: Thomas Y. Crowell, Co.
- *teaches the concept of zero, the numerals 1-12 and the concepts of groups and sets with illustrations of a growing village through the 12 months.*

Branley, Franklyn M. **How Little And How Much.** New York: Thomas Y. Crowell Co.
- *briefly introduces the use of scales to measure things, with emphasis on length and temperature.*

Carle, Eric. **The Very Hungry Caterpillar.** Ohio: Collins-World.
- *although not typically a counting book, this book can be used to teach both counting and the days of the week.*

Forte, Imogene, and MacKenzie, Joy. **Creative Math Experiences for the Young Child, Rev. Ed.** Nashville: Incentive Publications, Inc.
- *beginning concepts such as numerals, sets, sizes, shapes, time, money, measurements, fractions and math vocabulary are covered in this book.*

Froman, Robert. **Bigger and Smaller.** New York: Thomas Y. Crowell, Co.
- *helps explain the concept of size words (good for parent and teacher to share with a child).*

Lewin, Betsy. **Cat Count.** New York: Dodd, Mead & Co.
- *a rhyming accounting of cats, from 1 to 10, with a last minute addition from the fat, fun feline.*

Mack, Stan. **10 Bears in My Bed.** New York: Pantheon Books.
- *a goodnight countdown book that tells the tale of a little boy's attempt to get the bears out of his bed.*

Martin, Patricia Miles. **That Cat! 1-2-3.** New York: G.P. Putnam's Sons.
- *a cat knocks over a cardboard box and everything tumbles out by numerical sequence to 10.*

Sandak, Maurice. **One Was Johnny.** New York: Harper & Row.
- *a book from the nutshell library which teaches counting from 1 to 10 and backwards from 10 to 1.*

Taborin, Glorina. **Norman Rockwell's Counting Book.** New York: Harmony Books (Crown Pub.).
- *famous Rockwell paintings are paired with counting to 20.*

Wolff, Janet, and Owett, Bernard. **Let's Imagine Numbers!** New York: E.P. Dutton & Co., Inc.
- *through imagination, this book helps to make numbers more real to children and explores a world in which everything around us is a "number" of something.*

# FALL

| SUNDAY | MONDAY | TUESDAY | WEDNESDAY | THURSDAY | FRIDAY | SATURDAY |
|--------|--------|---------|-----------|----------|--------|----------|
|        |        |         |           |          |        |          |
|        |        |         |           |          |        |          |
|        |        |         |           |          |        |          |
|        |        |         |           |          |        |          |
|        |        |         |           |          |        |          |

**SEPTEMBER**

# SEPTEMBER

- Conduct a "Marvelous Me" study.

  Help the children make "Marvelous Me" booklets (use pages **16-21**, **25**, and **189**).

  Give each child a copy of page **46** to illustrate during the first week of school and again during the last week of school. Date each page and give them to parents at a family open house (see May activities) or on the last day of school.

  Read aloud and discuss "Billy Goes To School" (page **24**). Ask the children to talk about how they felt on the first day of school.

  Conclude the "Marvelous Me" study with pages **26-31**. Give awards to the children for tying shoes correctly. Invite another class to join in the teddy bear parade! (Note: Assure the children that any stuffed animal is fine. Have a few "extras" for those children who do not bring an animal from home.)

- Use the "Apple From The Teacher" bulletin board on page **23** as a welcome to school. Substitute the caption "Look Who's Here" and tape a picture of each student to an apple for the board. Ask the children to bring photographs from home, or use a Polaroid to take pictures in class. Later, change the caption to "Apple From The Teacher" and let each child turn over his or her apple to uncover the surprise for the day.

- Begin using the celebration tree (page **33**) this month. Help the children cut oval shapes out of colorful construction paper, punch holes in them, and thread yarn through the holes for hanging. Have each child draw a picture of one thing he or she likes about school on an oval shape. Hang the drawings on the celebration tree.

- Read *Ferdinand The Bull* and *Swimmy* (page **47**) to motivate discussion and promote acceptance of individual differences in people.

- Combine pages **61-65** from the language unit with pages **210-216** from the math unit to make a multi-disciplinary mini-unit for evaluating and reinforcing motor skills development.

- Reproduce the alphabet on page **77** and send it home with each child for parents to use as a guide when helping children at home.

- Set up and introduce the housekeeping center (page **15**). Ask the children to bring contributions from home. Establish rules for free time and for general use of the center.

- Be sure to use lots of awards during this first month of school. ("Showed Self-Control" page **285**, "My Teacher Is Proud Of Me" page **299**.)

| SUNDAY | MONDAY | TUESDAY | WEDNESDAY | THURSDAY | FRIDAY | SATURDAY |
|--------|--------|---------|-----------|----------|--------|----------|
|        |        |         |           |          |        |          |
|        |        |         |           |          |        |          |
|        |        |         |           |          |        |          |
|        |        |         |           |          |        |          |
|        |        |         |           |          |        |          |

**OCTOBER**

# OCTOBER

- Concentrate on numerals and number words. Read *That Cat! 1-2-3* and *One Was Johnny* (page **257**). Give each child copies of pages **222-244** for use as a group activity (pages **242-244** are for reinforcement). Discuss the graphic theme of each page as it is completed. Help the children make construction paper covers, punch holes in the pages, assemble the pages, and thread yarn through the holes to make "take-home booklets."

- Reproduce page **35** for each child. Assist the children in assembling the Halloween finger puppets. Use a cardboard box to make a stage for puppet plays to be composed and produced by the class. To extend this activity, help the children make other simple puppets by following the directions on pages **132-137**.

cut a
door for the puppeteers

- Plan a field trip to a supermarket, farm, or roadside stand if possible to select a pumpkin for the class jack-o'-lantern.

Involve the children in the removal of the seeds from the pumpkin before creating the jack-o'-lantern. Using felt-tip markers to draw the face as opposed to carving the face is safe and helps keep the pumpkin "sturdy" for a longer time.

See the recipe on page **36** for toasted pumpkin seeds. Serve the delicious pumpkin seeds with apple juice for a healthy and fun party snack.

Save a handful of seeds. Wash the seeds and plant them in a pot of soil. Place the pot in a sunny window and watch to see the new plants emerge!

Use the pumpkin for a science experience! Keep the pumpkin long after Halloween to observe what happens as the pumpkin begins to deteriorate. Discuss the whys and hows of the deterioration process. For example, ask the children to observe and discuss how and why the pumpkin changes in appearance, smell, and the way it feels to the touch.

Just for fun, use page **119** sometime during the pumpkin experience!

# NOVEMBER

| SUNDAY | MONDAY | TUESDAY | WEDNESDAY | THURSDAY | FRIDAY | SATURDAY |
|--------|--------|---------|-----------|----------|--------|----------|
|        |        |         |           |          |        |          |
|        |        |         |           |          |        |          |
|        |        |         |           |          |        |          |
|        |        |         |           |          |        |          |
|        |        |         |           |          |        |          |

# NOVEMBER

- Adapt the "I Am Thankful" work sheet on page **37** for the school setting. Ask the children to draw a person or situation in the school for which they are thankful such as the principal, the school secretary, a cafeteria worker, the nurse, assembly programs, etc. On the last day of school before the Thanksgiving holidays, have the class deliver their "messages" as a group.

- Tear autumn scenes from magazines to make puzzles to use in reinforcing visual perception skills (see page **55**). Reproduce and staple together pages **66-68** and page **79** (for review) to make a "take-home booklet" for each child. Include a brief note to parents with suggestions for home activities (see page **55**).

- Prepare an autumn leaves bulletin board display. Take the children outside to collect leaves for the board, or use the pattern on page **268** to cut leaves out of autumn colors of construction paper (you may also use the squirrel pattern on page **270**). Have the children make leaf rubbings with the leftover leaves (page **115**).

- Set up a science exploration center focusing on measurement. Place the measurement tools shown on page **253** in the center as well as a variety of jars (1 pt., 1 qt., ½ gal., 1 gal.), measuring spoons, a tape measure, and a yardstick. Prepare a chart with questions for the children to answer by experimenting. Make a place for books related to measurement such as *How Little And How Much* and *Bigger And Smaller* (page **257**). Use the ideas on pages **250-252** for group measurement activities, and reproduce pages **253** and **254** for each child's use. As a culminating activity, have the children use the measurement tools to help prepare a recipe from pages **170-172**.

Autumn Leaves are falling, falling
Red, green, gold and brown
Autumn leaves are falling, falling
Autumn leaves are falling down.

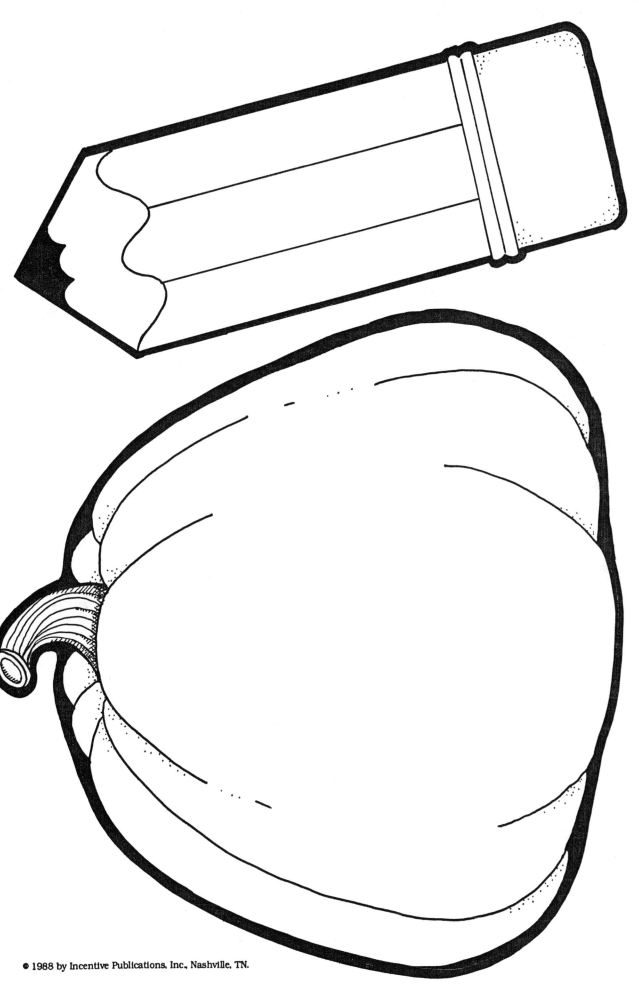

# I CAN COUNT ON YOU

TO: _____

FROM: _____

FOR: _____

DATE: _____

# THE INCHWORM AWARD

TO: _____

FROM: _____

FOR: _____

DATE: _____

# TELLING TIME AWARD

TO: _____

FROM: _____

FOR: _____

DATE: _____

| SUNDAY | MONDAY | TUESDAY | WEDNESDAY | THURSDAY | FRIDAY | SATURDAY |
|--------|--------|---------|-----------|----------|--------|----------|
|        |        |         |           |          |        |          |
|        |        |         |           |          |        |          |
|        |        |         |           |          |        |          |
|        |        |         |           |          |        |          |
|        |        |         |           |          |        |          |

**DECEMBER**

# DECEMBER

- Holiday time is sharing time. Set up a center for gift making, complete with all of the supplies and equipment needed to make a gift appropriate for a shut-in (see pages **122-125**). Discuss with the children the joy of giving rather than receiving. Plan a trip to a hospital or nursing home to deliver the children's handmade gifts. Another fun gift to make is a piñata for younger children at a day care center (page **128**). The children might enjoy making an extra piñata to break at their own holiday party!

- Just for fun, use the work sheet on page **38** as a motivator for a discussion of toys. Compare the toys enjoyed by boys and girls today with the toys once enjoyed by the children's parents. Ask the children to continue the discussion at home with family members.

- Being the first day of winter, December 22 is a good day to create "snowy day" pictures using soap suds finger paint and dark blue construction paper. Follow the directions on page **130** for making soap suds finger paint (omit the food coloring). After the children complete their pictures, read aloud *The Snowy Day* by Ezra Jack Keats (page **157**).

- To avoid the pre-holiday tension that tends to sabotage even the best of plans, involve the children in spontaneous movement activities such as the ones on pages **142-143**. Favorite singing games such as "Skip To My Lou," "The Noble Duke of York," and "The Farmer In The Dell" are good indoor relaxers. A small, carefully selected supply of musical activity records and/or cassette tapes is a sound investment for any teacher of young children.

- Revise the celebration tree for the holidays (see page **34**).

- To reinforce numeral/number skills, make activity packages using pages **222-241**. After reproducing the pages, cut the numeral/number strips off of the bottoms of the pages. Put the illustrated portion of each page in a Manila envelope and the numeral/number strips in another Manila envelope. Instruct the children to match the illustrations and the corresponding numeral/number strips by paper clipping them together. This activity may be used as a free choice interest center activity or a directed activity for individuals or small groups.

|  |  |  |  |  |  | SUNDAY |
|  |  |  |  |  |  | MONDAY |
|  |  |  |  |  |  | TUESDAY |
|  |  |  |  |  |  | WEDNESDAY |
|  |  |  |  |  |  | THURSDAY |
|  |  |  |  |  |  | FRIDAY |
|  |  |  |  |  |  | SATURDAY |

**JANUARY**

# JANUARY

- Celebrate National Handwriting Day (January 23) by having the children practice their writing skills (see pages **76** and **77**). Ask each child to write his or her name as neatly as possible on a sentence strip to be placed on a bulletin board with the heading "Name Games." Have the children play name games such as matching names and children, finding all of the names that begin with the same letter or that end with "e" or "y", etc. Let the children make up other name games of their own.

- Use pages **43** and **44** to introduce a study of community helpers. Invite various community workers to visit the class to discuss their roles. Plan at least one follow-up field trip to a community helper's work place (see pages **39** and **40**).

- Use the ideas, activities, and patterns on pages **191-193** as the basis of an experiential unit on sound. Place a bell, an alarm clock, pebbles in a tin can, two tin pie pans, etc. in the science corner for the children to use in experimenting with sound. Take the children on a listening walk (see page **174**). After returning from the walk, have the children draw pictures of the things they heard. Discuss "the sounds around us." Have the children imagine what it would be like if there were no sounds. Ask the children to try to be quiet and still for three minutes. Discuss the experience.

- A perfect study to follow the sound unit is a mini-unit on musical instruments. Set up a corner with pictures of various instruments as well as actual instruments. If possible, arrange to have one or more musicians visit the class to demonstrate how various instruments are played and how they sound. Help the children make their own instruments following the directions on pages **144-146**. Discuss the kinds of instruments that are found in concert bands, orchestras, and other kinds of musical ensembles. Read aloud *The Philharmonic Gets Dressed* by Karla Kuskin (page **157**) to conclude the study.

- Use pages **86-88** in combination with hands-on sequencing and classifying activities to reinforce beginning reading comprehension skills. Ask the children to classify leaves, toys, and hard candies by color, size, and shape. Cut apart simple comic strips and place them in an envelope for the children to arrange in sequence as a free choice activity.

# FEBRUARY

## I LOVE YOU

| SUNDAY | MONDAY | TUESDAY | WEDNESDAY | THURSDAY | FRIDAY | SATURDAY |
|--------|--------|---------|-----------|----------|--------|----------|
|        |        |         |           |          |        |          |
|        |        |         |           |          |        |          |
|        |        |         |           |          |        |          |
|        |        |         |           |          |        |          |
|        |        |         |           |          |        |          |
|        |        |         |           |          |        |          |

# FEBRUARY

● Have the children listen to weather forecasts several days before Groundhog Day (February 2) and make predictions about the groundhog and his shadow. Record the predictions on a chart to provide motivation for lively discussion. Role play the groundhog searching for his shadow. (Note: groundhog pattern on page **283**.)

● Help the children develop creative thinking and visualization skills using pages **92-93**, **102-105**, and **118-119** as individual or small group activities. If the children are not ready to complete these activities as pencil and paper activities, use the same or similar ideas and ask children to respond verbally. Sharing ideas in a group setting is fun as well as profitable.

● February is birthday month! Place a calendar in a special place in the room. Let each child mark his or her birthday in some unique way. (Be sure to use a calendar which includes the summer months.) Plan to have a class birthday party. Let the children make the decorations (paper plates, page **114**; balloons, page **115**). For added excitement, let the children select and prepare the food — it's perfectly fine to stray from the traditional cake and punch! (See pages **170-172**.)

● Valentine's Day is a fine time to study the postal system and its importance to daily life as well as individual differences in people. Have the children make collage valentines specially designed for special people. Let each child look through magazines and catalogs for pictures related to his or her special person. For example, grandmother likes to work in her flower garden, bake apple pies, ride horses, and watch television. A big brother likes cats, hot dogs, and football and wants to be an airline pilot one day. Have the children cut out the pictures and paste them on construction paper which has been folded down the middle. After the children write their valentine messages, help them seal the cards and write the addresses on the outsides. Plan a trip to the post office to buy stamps and mail the cards! (For an alternative idea, use the greeting card suggestions on page **124**.)

● To develop listening skills and extend attention spans, cover an easel or small bulletin board with felt or cotton flannel for use in storytelling, directed teaching, and free time activity center projects. Cut out the figures on page **137** and back them with felt, flannel, or Velcro strips. Tell the story of Little Red Riding Hood by moving the figures on the felt board. Other good stories to share in this way are "Jack and the Bean Stalk," "Hansel and Gretel," and "Goldilocks and the Three Bears."

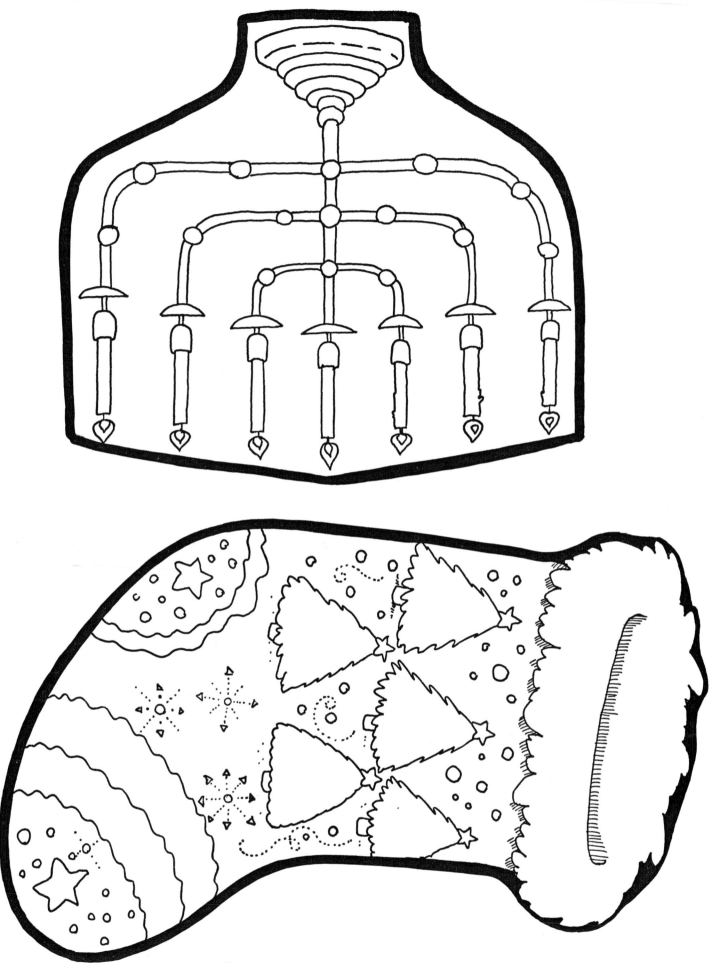

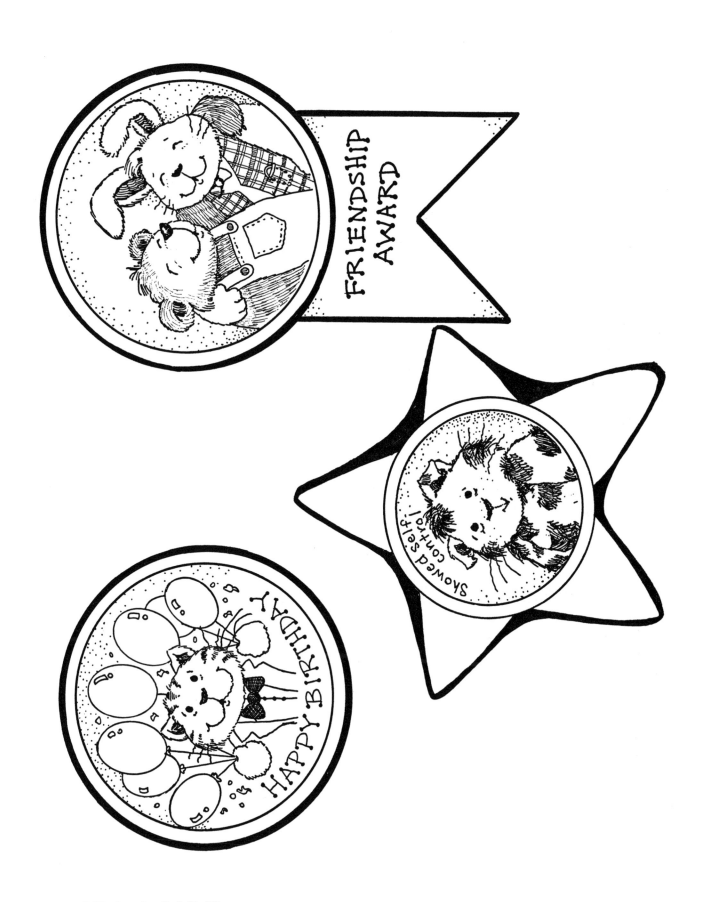

FRIENDSHIP AWARD

Showed self-control

HAPPY BIRTHDAY

# SPRING

| SUNDAY | MONDAY | TUESDAY | WEDNESDAY | THURSDAY | FRIDAY | SATURDAY |
|--------|--------|---------|-----------|----------|--------|----------|
|        |        |         |           |          |        |          |
|        |        |         |           |          |        |          |
|        |        |         |           |          |        |          |
|        |        |         |           |          |        |          |
|        |        |         |           |          |        |          |

**MARCH**

# MARCH

- Tell the children that March is National Peanut Month. Bring raw peanuts to class and allow the children to observe a peanut before and after it is shelled. Discuss how and where peanuts are grown as well as the many kinds of products made from peanuts. Let the children help to roast a portion of the peanuts. Ask the children to taste both roasted and raw peanuts and to note the differences in taste. See pages **30** and **171** for tasty peanut butter snacks.

- Read aloud *The Story of Johnny Appleseed* by Aliki (New Jersey: Prentice Hall, Inc.) on March 11, Johnny Appleseed Day. Provide each student with an apple or ask the children to bring apples from home. Help the children cut their apples and remove several seeds. Then have the children plant the seeds in pots of soil to be placed on a windowsill for observation. Substitute apples for the vegetables suggested in the animal critter activity on page **127** and help the children make apple critters.

- In like a lion, out like a lamb (patterns on page **295**). March is ideal for a study of the weather. Use pages **195-202** to plan a unit appropriate to the interest needs of the group. Be sure to include a weather calendar bulletin board (page **195**) and an outdoor session for the paper airplane activity on page **199**. Read aloud *Gilberto and The Wind* by Marie Hall Ets (page **203**) in observance of March winds!

- During National Poison Prevention Week (March 19-25), discuss the harmful effects of certain household products containing poisonous chemicals. Bring examples of such products to class for the children to become familiar with (be sure to empty the containers). Have the children make poison warning labels to tape to harmful household products in their own homes (page **41**).

- Celebrate St. Patrick's Day! Revise the celebration tree for St. Patrick's Day (page **34**) by using the shamrock pattern on page **296**. Have the children use the shamrock pattern to make their own shamrocks to wear on the 17th! Encourage the children to wear as much green as they can and to locate and describe green things in the classroom. Share the history and legends related to this special holiday.

- "Plant" grass or parsley seeds on a sponge (cut like a shamrock for St. Patrick's Day) and place the sponge in a shallow dish. In a few weeks, cut the grass with scissors instead of a lawn mower!

- Children will enjoy witnessing the first signs of spring as they explore the outdoors on a nature walk. See pages **173-174** for ideas for exploring and discovering the mysteries of nature. After returning from an outdoor excursion, read *When The Root Children Wake Up* by Helen Dean Fisk (page **203**).

| | | | | | SUNDAY |
|---|---|---|---|---|---|
| | | | | | MONDAY |
| | | | | | TUESDAY |
| | | | | | WEDNESDAY |
| | | | | | THURSDAY |
| | | | | | FRIDAY |
| | | | | | SATURDAY |

**APRIL**

# APRIL

- April showers bring May flowers! Refer to pages **197** and **198** for creative, fun-to-do rainy day activities. These activities are designed for use during or after a rain shower, so there should be many opportunities for each activity during the month. Include Alvin Tresselt's *Rain Drop Splash* (page **203**) in a rainy day reading session.

- Observe National Library Week (April 2-8).

  Take the children to a public library and arrange to have each child secure a library card if possible.

  Set aside time each day during the week for a special read-aloud session. The bibliographies on pages **47, 60, 106-107, 156-157, 203,** and **257** list many excellent books carefully selected for their appeal to young children. Involve the children in the selection of the "book for the day" if desired.

  Make bookmarks (page **100**) using felt or construction paper.

  Use page **98** or **99** as a homework project, requesting the children to complete one of the pages with an adult at home. Ask the children to bring their completed pages to school the next day for a group discussion. Post the pages on a bulletin board with the heading "We Love Books."

- Prepare a mini-unit on safety using the activities and ideas on page **41**. Stress bicycle safety in conjunction with Bicycle Safety Week (April 16-22). Present each student with a safety award (page **42**) at the end of the week.

- April is a month of rebirth, spring flowers, green grass, colorful eggs, and furry rabbits! Read aloud *The Tale of Peter Rabbit* by Beatrix Potter (page **60**) to celebrate spring.

- Use pages **179-187** as the kickoff for a unit on living things. Arrange a bulletin board display with the heading "Living and Non-living Things." Ask the children to look through magazines and catalogs to find pictures of living and non-living things to display on the appropriate sides of the board. If the children's attention span warrants an extension, include a mini-unit on the human body (page **188**) and nutrition (**189-190**).

- Bring some budding branches (apple, peach, or forsythia) to class. Place the branches in a pail of water and observe how the buds blossom.

| SUNDAY | MONDAY | TUESDAY | WEDNESDAY | THURSDAY | FRIDAY | SATURDAY |
|--------|--------|---------|-----------|----------|--------|----------|
|        |        |         |           |          |        |          |
|        |        |         |           |          |        |          |
|        |        |         |           |          |        |          |
|        |        |         |           |          |        |          |
|        |        |         |           |          |        |          |
|        |        |         |           |          |        |          |
|        |        |         |           |          |        |          |

**MAY**

HAPPY MOTHER'S DAY

RADISHES ZINNIAS CARROTS

# MAY

- Have a May Day festival! (On or near May 1.)

  Make a May pole by attaching different colors of crepe paper streamers to the top of a pole (flagpoles are excellent for this). Instruct each child to hold the end of one of the streamers and to weave in, out, and around one another according to your instructions. If you like, have the children walk around the pole to music.

  Help the children make May Day baskets (page **123**). Take the children for a walk around school grounds to collect spring flowers for their baskets.

  Stage a May Day scarf dance (page **139**). Take the children outdoors on a breezy day and have them imitate the spring wind as they follow the movements of their scarfs.

- May is the perfect time to conduct a bird watch study. Help the children make one or more birdhouses (see page **175**) to hang outside a classroom window. Children will delight in watching to see what kinds of birds choose to live there. Set up a bird exploration center (refer to pages **166-169**) where the children may go individually or in small groups to learn more about various birds.

- In observance of National Family Week (May 7-14), sponsor a family open house one afternoon or evening during the week. Have the children make personal invitations to take home to their families and encourage them to bring as many family members as they can. Name tags made from any of the patterns on pages **267-270, 281-285**, and **295-299** will add to the festivities. Allow the children to take their families on a tour of the classroom and to introduce them to one another.

- Reproduce copies of page **46** for the children to complete during the last week of school. Pair the pages with the copies of the same page which the children completed during the first week of school (see September activities). Give the pages to parents at the family open house or on the last day of school for a memento of the year.

- Have the children make coupon books for Mother's Day (page **124**). Take advantage of this opportunity to discuss family responsibilities with the children.

- Reproduce page **105** for each child and distribute the pages during International Pickle Week (May 18-27). Display the completed pages on a bulletin board or wall.

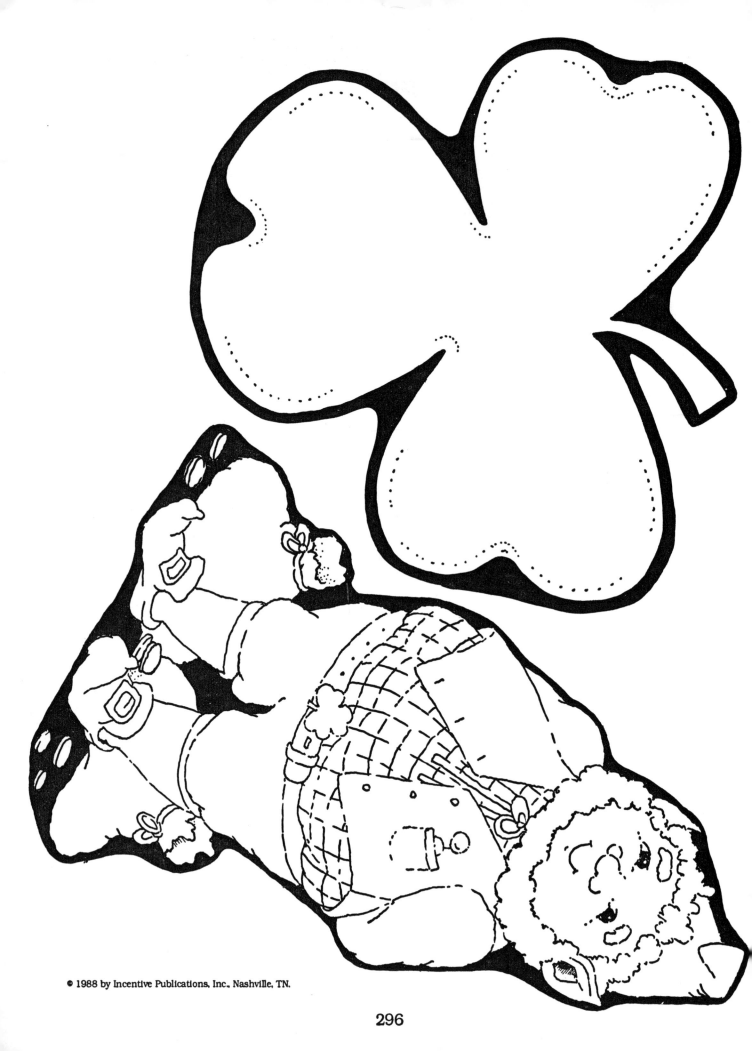

TO: _____

FOR:

Date: _____

MY TEACHER
IS PROUD
OF ME!
BECAUSE:

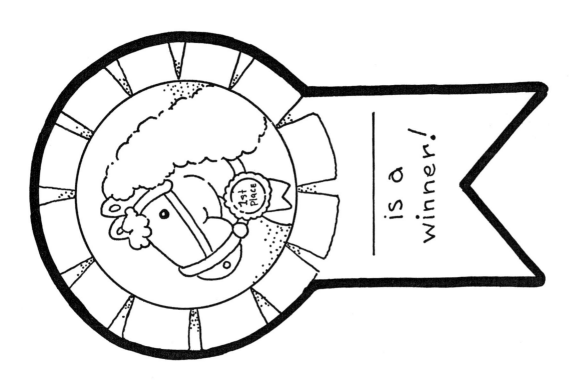

_____
is a
winner!

# INDEX